WHAT'S THE GOOD OF HUMANITY?

The Pro Ecclesia Series

Books in the Pro Ecclesia series are "for the Church." The series is sponsored by the Center for Catholic and Evangelical Theology, founded by Carl Braaten and Robert Jenson in 1991. The series seeks to nourish the Church's faithfulness to the gospel of Jesus Christ through a theology that is self-critically committed to the biblical, dogmatic, liturgical, and ethical traditions that form the foundation for a fruitful ecumenical theology. The series reflects a commitment to the classical tradition of the Church as providing the resources critically needed by the various churches as they face modern and post-modern challenges. The series will include books by individuals as well as collections of essays by individuals and groups. The Editorial Board will be drawn from various Christian traditions.

TITLES IN THE SERIES INCLUDE:

The Morally Divided Body: Ethical Disagreement and the Unity of the Church, edited by Michael Root and James J. Buckley

Christian Theology and Islam, edited by Michael Root and James J. Buckley

Who Do You Say That I Am?: Proclaiming and Following Jesus Today, edited by Michael Root and James J. Buckley

What Does It Mean to "Do This"?: Supper, Mass, Eucharist, edited by Michael Root and James J. Buckley

Heaven, Hell, . . . and Purgatory?, edited by Michael Root and James J. Buckley

Life Amid the Principalities: Identifying, Understanding, and Engaging Created, Fallen, and Disarmed Powers Today, edited by Michael Root and James J. Buckley

Remembering the Reformation: Commemorate? Celebrate? Repent?, edited by Michael Root and James J. Buckley

The Emerging Christian Minority, edited by Victor Lee Austin and Joel C. Daniels

Repentance and Forgiveness, edited by Matthew E. Burdette and Victor Lee Austin

What's the Good of Humanity?

Edited by

Victor Lee Austin
and Joel C. Daniels

CASCADE *Books* • Eugene, Oregon

WHAT'S THE GOOD OF HUMANITY?

Pro Ecclesia Series 10

Copyright © 2021 Wipf and Stock Publishers. All rights reserved. Except for brief quotations in critical publications or reviews, no part of this book may be reproduced in any manner without prior written permission from the publisher. Write: Permissions, Wipf and Stock Publishers, 199 W. 8th Ave., Suite 3, Eugene, OR 97401.

Cascade Books
An Imprint of Wipf and Stock Publishers
199 W. 8th Ave., Suite 3
Eugene, OR 97401

www.wipfandstock.com

PAPERBACK ISBN: 978-1-7252-5520-3
HARDCOVER ISBN: 978-1-7252-5521-0
EBOOK ISBN: 978-1-7252-5522-7

Cataloguing-in-Publication data:

Names: Austin, Victor Lee, editor. | Daniels, Joel C., editor.

Title: What's the good of humanity / edited by Victor Austin Lee and Joel C. Daniels.

Description: Eugene, OR : Cascade Books, 2021 | Series: Pro Ecclesia Series 10

Identifiers: ISBN 978-1-7252-5520-3 (paperback) | ISBN 978-1-7252-5521-0 (hardcover) | ISBN 978-1-7252-5522-7 (ebook)

Subjects: LCSH: Christianity. | Theological anthropology. | Christian ethics.

Classification: BL265.T4 W43 2021 (print) | BL265.T4 W43 (ebook)

Table of Contents

List of Contributors · vii

Preface · xi
VICTOR LEE AUSTIN AND JOEL C. DANIELS

1. Chastity and the Wealth of Life · 1
   PHILLIP CARY

2. Practicing Christianity in the Age of Technology · 16
   DONNA FREITAS

3. "Struck Down, but Not Destroyed..." · 28
   PAUL R. HINLICKY

4. Male and Female, the Image of God, and the Significance of Children · 33
   EDITH M. HUMPHREY

5. Body, Soul, Resurrection, and Heaven · 54
   PATRICK LEE

6. On Dying · 70
   GILBERT MEILAENDER

7. What Is the Relationship of the Brain, Consciousness, and Christian Faith? · 83
   NANCEY MURPHY

List of contributors

Victor Lee Austin, program director of the Center for Catholic and Evangelical Theology, is theologian-in-residence of the Episcopal Diocese of Dallas. His books include *Up with Authority*, *Christian Ethics: A Guide for the Perplexed*, *Losing Susan*, and *Friendship: The Heart of Being Human*.

Phillip Cary is professor of philosophy at Eastern University in Pennsylvania, where he is also scholar-in-residence at the Templeton Honors College and teaches in the Master of Arts in Teaching program for classical teachers. He is the editor of *Pro Ecclesia*, the journal of the Center of Catholic and Evangelical Theology. In addition to works on Augustine, a commentary on the book of Jonah, and a book on popular spirituality, his most recent book is *The Meaning of Protestant Theology: Luther, Augustine, and the Gospel That Gives Us Christ* (Baker Academic, 2019). He has also published lecture series with the Great Courses, including courses on Luther, Augustine, and the history of Christian theology.

Joel C. Daniels is rector of the Nevil Memorial Church of St. George in Ardmore, Pennsylvania, and postdoctoral fellow at the Center for Mind and Culture. He is the author of *Theology, Tragedy, and Suffering in Nature: Toward a Realist Doctrine of Creation*. His teaching ministry includes serving as adjunct faculty at Fordham University and the General Theological Seminary, as well as training those in formation for Holy Orders in the Episcopal Diocese of Pennsylvania. He is a member of the Society of Scholar-Priests.

Donna Freitas is the author of over twenty books, including *Sex and the Soul: Juggling Sexuality, Spirituality, Romance, and Religion*; *The Happiness Effect: How a Generation Is Trying to Appear Perfect at Any Cost*; and, most recently, *Consent on Campus: A Manifesto*, all from Oxford

University Press. She has written opinion pieces and articles based on her research for *The New York Times*, *The Wall Street Journal*, *The Washington Post*, and *The Boston Globe*, among other newspapers and magazines. She has appeared on other media outlets to discuss her work, from NPR's *All Things Considered* to *The Today Show*. Freitas is also the author of many works of fiction and creative nonfiction, including *Consent: A Memoir of Unwanted Attention*, which was released in September of 2019 from Little, Brown and Co. She lives in Brooklyn, New York.

Paul R. Hinlicky is Tise Professor at Roanoke College in Salem, Virginia, and a board member of the Center for Catholic and Evangelical Theology. Previously, he was visiting professor of systematic theology at the Protestant Theological Faculty of Comenius University in Bratislava. He is author of numerous theological studies, including *Paths Not Taken*, *Divine Complexity*, *Divine Simplicity*, *Luther and the Beloved Community*, *Before Auschwitz*, *Between Apocalyptic Theology and Humanist Philosophy*, *Luther for Evangelicals*, and a systematic theology, *Beloved Community: Critical Dogmatics after Christendom*. He is an ordained minister of the Evangelical Lutheran Church in America. With his daughter, theologian Sarah Hinlicky Wilson, he publishes a biweekly podcast titled *Queen of the Sciences* (see PaulHinlicky.com). With his wife, Ellen, and son, Will, he has a small farm in the mountains of West Virginia where he raises naturally grass-fed beef, chickens, and honeybees (see stgallfarm.com).

Patrick Lee holds the John N. and Jamie D. McAleer Chair of Bioethics and is the director of the Center for Bioethics at Franciscan University of Steubenville. He is the author of three books—*Body-Self Dualism in Contemporary Ethics and Politics*, with Robert P. George (2008), *Abortion and Unborn Human Life* (2010), and *Conjugal Union: What Marriage Is and Why It Matters*, with Robert P. George (2014)—and numerous scholarly and popular articles on bioethics and philosophical issues.

Edith M. Humphrey is the William F. Orr Professor of New Testament at Pittsburgh Theological Seminary, a member of St. Nicholas Orthodox Church (McKees Rock), and secretary for the Orthodox Theological Society of America from 2016 to 2019. Married to her husband, Chris, for forty-four years, she is mother to three daughters and sons-in-law, and grandmother to nineteen grandchildren. A frequent speaker in various Christian contexts, she is the author of numerous articles and eight books on topics as diverse as apocalypses, worship, Christian spirituality, human sexuality, and C. S. Lewis. She wrote the foreword to the latest edition of Fr. Schmemann's *For the Life of the World*, recently completed a novel for middle-school children in which they travel in time and space to meet their name-saints, and is writing a book on the topic of mediation.

Gilbert Meilaender is senior research professor at Valparaiso University where, prior to retirement, he held the Duesenberg Chair in Christian Ethics. Among his books are *Friendship: A Study in Theological Ethics*; *The Way That Leads There: Augustinian Reflections on the Christian Life*; and *Not by Nature but by Grace: Forming Families through Adoption*. He is coeditor (with William Werpehowski) of the *Oxford Handbook of Theological Ethics*. Meilaender's work in the area of bioethics is well known. He is a fellow of the Hastings Center and was a member of the President's Council on Bioethics from 2002 to 2009.

Nancey Murphy is senior professor of Christian philosophy at Fuller Seminary in Pasadena, California. She is the author of ten books and the coeditor of twelve. Her first book, *Theology in the Age of Scientific Reasoning* (Cornell, 1990), won the American Academy of Religion Award for Excellence in 1992. Other books include *Did My Neurons Make Me Do It? Philosophical and Neurobiological Perspectives on Moral Responsibility and Free Will* (with W. S. Brown) and *Downward Causation and the Neurobiology of Free Will* (with G. F. R. Ellis and T. O'Connor). Her most recent book is *A Philosophy of the Christian Religion for the Twenty-First Century* (SPCK, 2018).

Preface

Explorations and Articulations of Christian Wisdom

IT IS NOT HARD to find worry, indeed anxiety, about the corrosive effects of technology upon people today. Studies that not long ago would have been rejected as crankish are now front-page news, or perhaps we should say, regular occupants of news feeds. Is screen time harming children? Are our brains being rewired, through electronic stimuli, to think differently? Has technology made our civil discourse radioactive? Such anxiety is undeniably now part of the cultural milieu. There are also the questions about longer-term trends. We ponder the effects of technology on what we consider as normal human beings and normal human relationships, from contraception, to designer babies, to performance-enhancing drugs, and so forth. We could worry, and perhaps we should worry, about the relationship of technology and what is called "social capital," and particularly the poverty of those who lack networks of social relationship.

This is the context for the present volume, and such questions are, and should be, present throughout the essays. But they are not the primary focus. All of these anxieties are particular forms of a general fear, a fear that true humanity is slipping away from us. And so, the most basic question is not what we might be losing, but what true humanity is in the first place. What does it mean to be human?

In our cultural moment, it is important that we can articulate Christian wisdom about the good of humanity. The good comes first; the positive comes before the negative. In the short run, an angry prophet (or pseudo-prophet) can draw a crowd and garner support by appealing to fear and stirring outrage. But such strategies will not last—and especially today are not likely to be persuasive. Rather, they simply fuel the perception that Christians are naysayers, dour and negative people.

On the contrary, the authors of the following essays help us to grasp the beauty and difficulty of Christian wisdom concerning human beings: drawing from Scripture and from science, they discuss how we might think about the soul and the body (the brain); about our finitude and mortality; about male and female and children; about human practices such as chastity, the accumulation of wealth, and, yes, the consumption of social media and the effects of smartphones. Our hope is that these essays will leave us better equipped to articulate, and thus give witness to, the good of humanity.

Victor Lee Austin, Episcopal Diocese of Dallas
Joel C. Daniels, Nevil Memorial Church of St. George

1

Chastity and the Wealth of Life

Phillip Cary

IN THE BOOK OF Genesis, no one goes shopping. I think that has something to do with our present-day confusions about sexuality. Let me try to explain.

Natural Law and Biblical Narrative

I am thinking in rather traditional terms, both about the biblical narrative and about human nature. In fact, I want to understand the connections between the Genesis narrative and what many theologians like to call "natural law." I am more of a narrative theologian myself, but I think the natural law theorists are on to something, and I want to see how that is connected to the shape of the narratives in Genesis, those old, old stories about people who are, after all, in a great many ways profoundly different from us, living without our technology, communications media and advanced economy. So it is always an important hermeneutical question: how much of the shape of this story is still the shape of *our* story? How much *should* it be? What do we learn about being human from a story where no one even thinks of going shopping? It's a different world, for sure.

And yet not so different. That's the intuition that brings natural law theories and readings of Genesis together. It used to be easier to do that than it is now. Theologians in my generation learned that we didn't have to read the first chapter of the Bible literally (we didn't have to be six-day creationists) but we agreed that something both profound and obvious was being said in Genesis 1:28 where we read: "Male and female he created them." Today, the meaning of that text remains profound, but it does not seem quite so obvious. There are alternatives, after all. Male and female—is that really necessary? It's not even always the case: there are intersex people (the I in LGBTQIA), people who might once have been called hermaphrodites, whose sex is biologically ambiguous, neither quite male nor quite female. And of course, nowadays we all know there are people who want to transition from male to female or vice-versa. And this is connected, at least politically, with forms of sexual desire that break the mold of what is nowadays called "heteronormativity," forms of desire that do not show up in Genesis, though Paul knows something about them and says they are "against nature" in the first chapter of Romans—one of the few phrases in the Bible that seem to be referring explicitly to something like natural law, which is to say the normative consequences of human nature—of the conception of human beings as *having* a nature that is not merely a normal thing but a normative thing, a way of being ourselves that is a way we *ought* to be.

The Primal Blessing

But, as I say, none of that seems obvious nowadays. I want to think about why that is, what that has to do with a culture where we are all shoppers and what the Genesis stories might be showing us that we're missing. I'll start with a standard connection in traditional sexual ethics. Natural law theorists in the Catholic tradition like to talk about the unitive good and the procreative good of marriage, and the connection between them. A "good," in this sense, is an end, a *telos* in Greek, the inherent goal of a natural process or structure: the answer to the question, "What's the good of it?" It's not hard to spot these two goods in the Genesis narrative. First, there's the procreative good that we share with the other animals: "Be fruitful and multiply." This is what will lead me to speak of "the wealth of life" in a moment. I think it's important that it is introduced as a blessing. Verbally, it has the form of a command, but Genesis tells us it is how God blesses us; indeed, it is the very first blessing mentioned in the Bible, addressed initially to creatures of the sea and sky, the fish in the water and the birds of the air, and then on the sixth day to human beings.

It has the *form* of a command, but it is in fact a blessing: a must in the service of a may. It is unlike a commandment because the difference between obedience and disobedience does not seem to arise. The narrative proceeds on the assumption that all living creatures *like* this blessing and are eager to do what God has said. Later in the narrative there are problems carrying out what God has said, as we hear of a series of women described as "barren," like soil in which seed does not germinate, but this is not a problem of disobedience, as if human beings did not desire to be fruitful and multiply as much as the beasts of the field and the birds of the air and the fish of the sea desire it. We are in a different social world from Genesis when people don't want to have children, or when celibacy shows up as a Christian vocation. Martin Luther's argument against a celibate priesthood pointed to the power of this blessing, which works mightily in us, willy-nilly, as the word of God is apt to do.[1]

So there are various ways we can resist this blessing, but by nature we do seem to like it. This is evidently connected with the next part of the blessing: all these creatures, fish and birds, male and female, and human beings as well, are to be fruitful and multiply so that they may "fill the waters" and "fill the earth." The word of God blesses them all with fruitfulness so that they may fill the world with good things. The notion is echoed in the description of the wealth of a house in the book of Proverbs, using the same verb:

> By wisdom a house is built
> And by understanding it is established
> By knowledge the rooms are *filled*
> With all precious and pleasant riches. (Prov 24:3-4)

Wisdom builds, understanding establishes, knowledge fills—and the result is riches in the house. This is comparable to God's work in creation, as we can see in the parallel verses earlier in Proverbs:

> The LORD by wisdom founded the earth
> By understanding he established the heavens
> By his knowledge the deeps broke open
> And the clouds drop down the dew. (Prov 3:19-20)

The wisdom of God founds the earth we walk on, the understanding of God establishes the heavens themselves under which we live, and his

---

1. See the opening argument in Martin Luther, "The Estate of Marriage," in *Luther's Works* (Philadelphia: Fortress, 1962), 45:18-19.

knowledge opens up the depths so that water springs forth from the earth just as it drops down from heaven, so that the earth is watered—so that it can be fruitful and filled with good things like a house filled with all pleasant riches and wealth.

Blessing in the Bible often means wealth, not least in Genesis. Think of how Jacob comes back from a far country blessed with flocks and herds and children, the fundamental form of wealth in that ancient pastoral culture. Wealth for these biblical people means living things that have been fruitful and multiplied, and have filled the household with good things. That is the first thing I have in mind when I speak of the wealth of life: the proliferation of living things, healthy, flourishing, fruitful and multiplying and filling the earth with good things—and first of all with themselves. That is the primal blessing of Genesis, the first blessing God has given to human beings when he created them.

Later, as man and woman are in exile from the primal garden, we find that the blessing is not inevitable. The narrative in Genesis in fact focuses on men and women who do not seem capable of being fruitful together and multiplying, like barren fields in which no seed can grow. And later still in the biblical narrative there are all manner of men and women who do not seem at all blessed, lacking this or that good of creation: the blind and the deaf, the ill and the lame, the kind of people to whom Jesus our Lord announces the kingdom of God by doing signs and wonders that restore to them the blessings and goods of creation. Much of the way we judge the justice of a community has to do with how the people within it who lack some of the natural goods of creation are treated, and whether this looks at all like the kingdom our Lord announces. This, I suppose, gives us a way of thinking about intersex people, who would be among those whom our Lord describes as being born eunuchs from their mother's womb, but who are not thereby excluded from the kingdom of God (Matt 19:12). He is perhaps thinking of the promise the LORD made through the prophet Isaiah, that to the eunuchs "who choose the things that please me and hold fast my covenant, I will give in my house and within my walls a monument and a name better than sons and daughters" (Isa 56:4).

What I want to think about in this essay, however, is what happens when we no longer regard sons and daughters, being fruitful and multiplying, as obvious blessings. In our culture they are a lifestyle choice, and one treated often with a certain amount of suspicion, for if indulged in—say, by begetting a large family—they are likely to get in the way of living a more creative and successful life. Having a big, growing family is at best a personal preference that mustn't be imposed on people and at worst the source of all sorts of social problems. Or so most people in our society are inclined to think. Therefore, I want to ask: what happens when it is no longer obvious to us that the primal blessing is—to use the natural law language—a natural good, inherently desirable for human beings as such? What have we lost in a culture which, on the contrary, makes it seem obvious to many of us that this is not a natural blessing but an unwanted burden to be avoided because it is an obstacle to our life plans and the success that we ought to desire?

Here I think the biblical narrative is getting at something deeper than what the natural law theory has the resources to say. For there is something more than natural about the good of procreation, which is why it is not merely a good but a divine blessing. As you may know, the Hebrew verb for "create" is never used of anyone but God. The Bible—followed by Western culture up to the eighteenth century—never speaks of human beings, or anything other than God, as "creative." Only God creates. Unless I am mistaken, you will not find that English verb used of anyone but God until late in the eighteenth century.

The Bible does not think that way, I take it, because in biblical thinking only God can bring new beings into being. Passing over some deep theological controversies, let me say that I think the theological tradition gets this right: only God brings new beings out of nothing. We who are made in the image of God can be makers, artists who make things out of other things, making pots out of clay, houses out of stone and wood, music out of sounds, and poetry out words (poetry, from a Greek word *poiein*, meaning "to make"—so that Middle English, which called poets "makers," was running parallel to ancient Greek). We are makers, but not creators. We cannot bring new things into being out of nothing.

And yet there is a deep way that we do bring new beings into being: we do not create, but we do procreate. Sharing the same blessing as the fish of the sea, the birds of the air and the beasts of the field, we can be fruitful and multiply, and fill the earth with good things, the wealth of new life. We can bring about and enjoy the procreative good. That is what the primal blessing does: it is the Word of God bestowing upon his creatures the power to bring forth new beings in their own image, after their kind. It is God giving a share of his creative power to us who are not creators but procreators, able by his gift to bring new beings into being, not out of nothing, but out of the material of our own united bodies.

Connecting Two Goods

And that, of course, brings me to the unitive good, the second good of marriage identified by natural law theorists and explicitly mentioned, as we all know, in the second chapter of Genesis, where the man recognizes his wife as his partner and ally, the helper who unlike all other creatures is suitable to him, as "bone of my bones, flesh of my flesh." And the narrative comments: Therefore a man leaves his father and his mother and cleaves to his woman, and they become one flesh.

I should perhaps say something about that word "helper." This is not a word for someone who helps you around the house, the hired help or servant who sweeps up after you. If you have the older and more precise translations of the Bible ringing in your ears and your memory, you may recognize it as a word of power. The helper or help mentioned most often in the Bible is God. "I will lift up my eyes to the hills," says the psalmist: "from whence cometh my help? My help cometh from the LORD, who made heaven and earth" (Ps 121:1–2). More than a dozen times in the Psalms, the LORD is our helper, and we pray to him: "Make haste to help me" (Ps 40:3). When the word is used of human beings, which is actually less often, it typically refers to military allies, the kind of people who come to your aid in the middle of the battle and turn the tide (e.g., Josh 10:6; 2 Sam 10:11; 1 Chr 12:17). In other words, "helper" refers to a kind of strength you need, without which you will die. That is what it means to be the woman in Genesis. Without her, Adam has no future, no progeny, his seed falls on the earth and dies and becomes nothing. Without the woman, the man's future is death. With her, it is life. That is why she is called "the Mother of all Living" (Gen 3:20).

So God in the beginning gives to human beings these two fundamental goods, according to their kind, which is to say according to their nature (in fact "kind" is the original English term for nature, as we can still see in the old term "mankind," and that sense of the term still lingers in the phrase "after their kind" used in Gen 1). There's the procreative good, by which they are fruitful and multiply, and the unitive good, by which the two become one flesh. Strikingly, the narrative leaves it up to us to make the connection between the two goods. The connection is, perhaps, not quite as natural as we might think. But the natural law theorists get this, as they routinely expound the procreative good as including not just the begetting of children but their education, child-raising in all its many facets: the human cultural activity that makes these living things that come from our bodies flourish as beings created in the image of God. We cannot enrich a human household with the wealth of life without wisdom, and understanding, and knowledge, as we have read already in the book of Proverbs. Properly connecting the unitive good and the procreative good is thus the first and fundamental responsibility of human wisdom and culture, following from the first of all God's blessings to human nature.

Chastity

Chastity is part of that wisdom, which is the responsibility of human culture and education. Chastity is the virtue that promotes the wealth of life by protecting the connection between the unitive good and the procreative good. It is not the same thing as celibacy, for it is a virtue that belongs within marriage as well as outside it. And within marriage itself is it more than merely fidelity or faithfulness, which is an important virtue that characterizes many other kinds of relationships in addition to marriage. You can be a faithful friend as well as a faithful spouse. What is unique about the virtue of chastity is that it aims to protect the connection between the unitive good and the procreative good. It brings male and female together sexually only as husband and wife, so that together they may become mother and father, and it refuses other uses of sexuality that disrupt that connection. It means that *this* man cleaves to *this* woman so as to be mother and father together: the same man who is one flesh with this woman becomes the father of her children, and she becomes the mother of his children, so that together they may be heads of a household that is filled with the wealth of life. The prohibitions and refusals that are necessary to chastity serve this positive connection between sex and family, making male and female into father and mother—which is to say, these two who become one flesh are not just means of passing on genes to the next generation but founders of a family, being fruitful and multiplying and filling not only the earth but the household with good things, the best things of all things there are on earth: the living creatures made in the image and likeness of God. That is the deepest way we share in the creativity of God, who established the heavens and the earth by his wisdom.

Chastity is not a word used in Genesis, but you can see chastity doing its work there, guarding the connection between the pairing of male and female, and the pairing of mother and father. God is the one who guards the connection most jealously, as he sends plagues upon Pharaoh because he has taken Sarai, Abram's wife, into his house (Gen 12:15–17), and nearly kills Abimelech for doing the same thing (Gen 20:3). And although Jacob, with his two wives and two concubines, is hardly a model of chastity, we can see a kind of critique of polygamy already in Genesis, when the wealth of Jacob's household, derived from the fruitfulness of the women he has acquired in his overreaching ambition, ends up in a kind of civil war among his diverse children—children of four mothers—who gang up on Joseph, the son of Rachel, the only woman Jacob is said to love. The murderous jealousy of the brothers reflects the frustrated jealousy of the four women competing for the love of one man, which is an explicit theme in the life of Leah, Rachel's sister (Gen 29:30–33). Failures of chastity—in this case clearly Jacob's failure—mean that something goes wrong in the household, and the flourishing of life can become deadly hatred. When Joseph's brothers convince their father, Jacob, that Joseph is dead, Jacob says this will bring him down in mourning to Sheol, the land of the dead, and he refuses to be comforted (Gen 37:35). He cannot reconcile himself to the fruit of his own unchastity. The brothers themselves are terrified, after Jacob's death, that Joseph will take vengeance on them all, and it is only Joseph's recognition of the overriding providence of God that points the way to their salvation, as he famously interprets their own story: "You meant it for evil against me, but God meant it for good, to bring it about that many people should be kept alive, as they are to this day" (Gen 50:20). The failure of chastity is sin, and the wages of sin is death, which can only be overcome by a power of life that is greater even than the primal blessing of procreation: a divine gift that turns us from death into life. A blessing of life greater than sex and procreation announces itself here at the end of Genesis, a blessing great enough to overcome sin and death.

In the story of sin and redemption that the Bible tells, a great many things go wrong after the disobedience of the man and his wife in the garden, not least of which is the precariousness of the primal blessing, as so many women in the story are barren for a long time, and something more than natural must happen for them to be fruitful. The ultimate wealth of life, which is life everlasting, requires something more than sex and procreation and marriage can give us. As a result, the biblical narrative is complex, subtle and often deeply ironic—not the kind of story that makes an easy Sunday school lesson—so we will not be able to read simple moral lessons right off its surface. (Jacob has the blessing of God because he trusts and obeys God, right? Well, not exactly.) Still, to follow the story and its ironies one does need a clear grasp of the virtues and vices that are at work in its characters, and why the virtues lead to life and the vices to death. For the rest of this essay, therefore, I want to step back from the details to look at some features of the story that provide the backdrop of the stage on which these virtues and vices play out. They are features that are obvious once you look at them, but they're easy to overlook.

The Original Economics

So back to the observation with which I began: in the book of Genesis, no one goes shopping. This is a key feature of the economics of Genesis, which is to say, its presentation of the wealth of life. The wealth of life fills the household with good things. That's a connection built into the very word "economy," *oikonomia* in Greek, meaning originally "household management," from *oikos*, household, and *nomos*, law, regularity, ordering or management. The term gets translated in the New Testament, in the King James, as either "stewardship" or "dispensation," the latter when it refers to God's providential management of the history of the world (Eph 1:10), that house that he founded by his wisdom, established by his understanding and enriched by his knowledge (Prov 24:3). The person put in charge of such a dispensation or management is an *oikonomos*, usually translated "steward." Hence Paul speaks of the stewardship or dispensation entrusted to him (1 Cor 9:17; cf. Eph 3:10 and Col 1:25), and describes the ministers of Christ as stewards of the mysteries of God (cf. 1 Cor 4:1; cf. Titus 1:7 and 1 Pet 4:10). A steward is the kind of servant who is given a couple of talents by the master of a household and told to get to work with them so that they are multiplied. The result of good stewardship, *oikonomia*, is that the wealth of life increases: the household flourishes, everybody gets enough to eat, flocks and herds multiply, crops and fields are fruitful. For one of the tasks of stewardship is to distribute food in the household (cf. Luke 12:42), so that living things in the household are healthy and flourishing; and one of the things you can do with a talent of silver is buy a fruitful field.

Let me at this point say a good word for the blessing of wealth. We have all sorts of problems with wealth, of course, especially when it is unjustly distributed. But wealth itself is unequivocally a good thing, a blessing. That's unmistakable in how Genesis uses the word for "blessing" and how it describes wealth. Both in the stories of Genesis and in the parables of Jesus (particularly in Luke, where the terms *oikonomia* and *oikonomos* are used in chapter 16), wealth is whatever makes a household flourish with healthy living bodies: well-fed children, flocks and herds on the increase, granaries filled. A household without wealth is one where children go hungry and die. So responsible householders and their stewards do not despise or avoid wealth but desire it; they are, as we rightly say, good providers. There is in this regard such a thing as too much of a good thing, but the thing that there's too much of is nonetheless a good thing. Ask anyone living in poverty with hungry children. Remembering the poor means not despising wealth but honoring their need for it.

So wealth means that living things flourish in the household, in the *oikos*. But think now how the meaning of "the economy" has changed for us. When we think of economics today, we do not typically think of living things. Even though our need, as living things, for food, shelter, and other necessities of subsistence is clearly at the foundation of economic activity, it's not what we now call "the bottom line." And we don't think of economics as fundamentally a household activity—though in Genesis it clearly is. No one goes shopping in Genesis. No market shows up in the story. Now this is striking, because ancient Near Eastern towns and villages surely had markets. Villages always have markets. But Genesis never mentions them. I think we should assume that the production of wealth by Abraham and Sarah, as well as their children and grandchildren, took place mainly in the household, through various household crafts, as well as the fundamental activity of pastoral care, in its original sense: watching over flocks and herds in their pastures, as they are fruitful and multiply and provide the household with the riches of healthy living things.

The Market Economy

That is not *our* economics. Our theories of economics in fact belong to a discipline originally called *political* economy, when it took shape in the eighteenth century in Adam Smith's epochal treatise on the wealth of *nations*. This was not at all the first treatise ever written on economics. We have a treatise on *oikonomia* attributed to Aristotle, and another attributed to Xenophon. In these treatises economics is in fact the study of the life of the household, the *oikos*, as politics is the study of the life of the city, the *polis*. Political economy would have been something like a contradiction of terms for Aristotle, or a category mistake. Economics is about the *oikos*, not the *polis*. So there is a decisive shift when economics comes to treat the wealth of nations rather than the wealth of the household, as if the fundamental place of economic activity is outside the household, in the market, where the wealth of nations is generated. The world is different when you have to go shopping to get what you need. Economics, like "creativity," has less and less to do with the procreation and the flourishing of living creatures and more and more to do with the activity of the marketplace.

Indeed, one consequence of the new economics—I will call it by the familiar name of "the market economy"—can be seen in the first professor of political economy in the English-speaking world, one of the great economists of the generation after Adam Smith: Robert Malthus, the man who gave us the Malthusian warning that the wealth of a nation is put under an intolerable strain by too many people being fruitful and multiplying.[2] Population increase becomes an economic danger rather than the form taken by the primal economic blessing of the human household. Malthus ended up urging that the lower classes should abstain altogether from marriage and family. Later, of course, the Malthusian impulse, as we could call it, welcomed contraception as a means of population control. We are products of Malthusian culture when we immediately associate large families with poverty and squalor and listless women, barefoot and pregnant. That picture inhabiting our minds is Malthusianism at the level of popular culture.

But with a little effort we can now see ironies that might have surprised Robert Malthus. We can see the great demographic crisis of contemporary Europe as the under-population of ethnic Europeans, who are not reproducing themselves at replacement rate. We can see an economic crisis on the horizon as too few young people shoulder the burden of supporting too many old people who were not fruitful and did not multiply. You can't produce adequate wealth without adequate population.

This irony is a result of what I take to be a fundamental feature of the culture of the market economy in the modern world: it instills in

---

2. For a good introduction with commentary, see the Norton Critical Edition of Thomas Robert Malthus, *An Essay on the Principle of Population*, ed. Philip Appleman (New York: Norton, 1976).

us the desire to be consumers and producers, but not procreators. Economic productivity comes first; that is what we are taught to call "success" and "creativity." The procreative good is recognized, but it is treated, by default, as a kind of burden to be avoided, except when you're "ready." Of course, by the time you're "ready," perhaps in your forties, you may need very modern technological assistance to procreate—something to do what only God can do for those barren old women in Genesis. But the market economy does step in here, with an expensive technology that is an important part of the economics of our health care system. For the procreative good can be separated from the unitive good in both directions: contraception can aim to give us the unitive good without the burden of the procreative good, and reproductive technologies increasingly aim to give us the procreative good with minimal contribution from the unitive good. I am thinking, of course, of in vitro fertilization and surrogate mothers. And if the news about successful human cloning in China is true, then the connection has already been completely severed, in at least one case.

In training us to separate the unitive good from the procreative good, the modern market economy trains us for unchastity. It produces a culture in which chastity starts looking not only old-fashioned but irrational, repressive and unjust, an unfair burden for young people, especially for women—for whom abortion is a human right—and for almost any "sexual minority." It makes it hard for us even to imagine chastity as a virtue, a good way for the soul to be formed. Hostility to the connection between the two goods has many motives, but let me highlight just one. The connection between man and wife and father and mother was at the heart of the old cultures in the West of patriarchy and monarchy and hierarchy, systems of authority and honor that liberal modernity opposes, often quite plausibly in the name of freedom, but also quite unmistakably to the benefit and enhancement of the market economy—*economic* freedom, as we have learned to call it.

Three Convictions

One crucial requirement for an ethics that recovers an understanding of the virtue of chastity for our time, I suggest, is to recognize the truth in the liberal claims on behalf of freedom, but peel them off from the interests of the modern market economy that they often serve. That is a big project, and I think it can only be carried out by intellectually engaged communities pursuing something like what Rod Dreher, picking up on a famous phrase by Alasdair MacIntyre, calls "the Benedict Option."[3] That's a long discussion in itself. Let me conclude here by simply gesturing in the direction of three countercultural convictions that I believe will be important for communities pursuing this option, and for churches that aim to recover a sense of the meaning of chastity in our time. These are convictions that should form our children's souls, I think, and which the ideals of success dangled in front of them by the modern market economy will attempt to undermine (and often, alas, *will* undermine). This is a cultural struggle, not a recipe. The convictions, if I am right, should give shape to a culture that brings us just a bit closer to what the Genesis stories, with all their narrative surprise and complexity and irony, take for granted as obvious features of our lives as sexual beings. These gestures of mine are, in effect, part of an attempt to begin imagining what *obedience* to biblical norms of sexuality amounts to in our time.

First, we should celebrate and support families, especially large families. Lots of churches are pretty good at this already, so this is a good place to start. Procreation is a blessing that can indeed be burdensome, so let us bear one another's burdens in this regard, and especially the burdens of young mothers. Let us support ways of working and living that conform to a woman's natural life cycle, which involves bearing children relatively young—in her twenties, not her forties—and going on to other kinds of work at a later time in her life than a man usually does—rather than running the same rat race as an ambitious young man and finding herself "ready" to become a mother only when it is biologically almost too late.

Second, let us teach our children that it is a blessing to be a mother, and that the possibility of this blessing makes an essential and blessed difference between women and men. It is far more important than merely

---

3. Rod Dreher, *The Benedict Option: A Strategy for Christians in a Post-Christian Nation* (New York: Penguin Random House, 2017). The title derives from the famous final sentences of Alasdair MacIntyre, *After Virtue*, 2nd ed. (Notre Dame: University of Notre Dame Press, 1984): "What matters at this stage is the construction of local forms of community within which civility and the intellectual and moral life can be sustained through the new dark ages which are already upon us. . . . [T]he barbarians are not waiting beyond the frontiers; they have already been governing us for quite some time. And it is our lack of consciousness of this that constitutes part of our predicament. We are waiting not for a Godot, but for another—doubtless very different—St. Benedict" (261).

psychological differences that are statistically present between statistical samples of women and men, and is indeed quite likely the biological source of those psychological differences, which are comparatively superficial, relative to the immense fact of the possibility of a woman's bodily participation in the blessing of being fruitful and multiplying. To celebrate this blessing and the sexual difference that follows from it, the fundamental difference between male and female, means resisting a certain mistaken kind of liberal egalitarianism, one which focuses on equality of outcome rather than equality of opportunity. I am thinking liberalism really is right to insist, against the old patriarchal culture, on the equality of women and men when it comes to the opportunities of participation in the market economy. But I am expecting that precisely this equality of opportunity will result in an inequality of outcome. Women who find the blessing in motherhood will often—not always, but very often—prefer to be mothers rather than to fight for success in the market economy, and will seek the procreative good before seeking the goods of the market economy, including a successful career as well as consumer goods. We should encourage and celebrate this, rather than join the culture of the modern market economy which trains us to think of these women as failing to truly fulfill themselves. There is a deep cultural struggle here, and the most important element in the struggle will be happy mothers with flourishing families.

That means, thirdly, that fatherhood, too, must be seen as a blessing. Happy young mothers need young men who are eager to be chaste husbands and faithful fathers, in contrast to the kind of young man who thinks of marriage as the way a man loses his freedom. The task of forming the souls of such young men will have us fighting upstream against very strong cultural currents. Let me conclude by trying to put my finger on one of them.

It used to be—still within living memory—that "responsible sexuality" meant sexuality within marriage, sexuality that respected the norms of chastity. Now our children are taught that responsible sexuality means sexuality with contraception. It is not just that contraception is permitted, it has become normative. In effect, responsible sex is sterile sex, sex that disconnects the unitive good from the procreative good. It fulfills what I will call "the fornicator's desire," which is the desire for sex without procreative consequences. This new and now current notion of responsible sexuality, which makes the fornicator's desire normative, is a cultural development that both Protestants and Catholics can and should oppose. You can take the usual Protestant view that contraception can be a legitimate way for married couples to regulate their fertility, while rejecting the much stronger notion that contraception is necessary for responsible sexuality. The ethicists, both Protestant and Catholic, who originally rejected contraception a century ago as immoral were on to something. To make contraception normative is to make what used to be called immorality—the fornicator's desire—into the normative form of sexuality. This, I think, is another "freedom" that serves not the legitimate aims of modern liberalism (of which there are many) but the functioning of the modern market economy, which needs a large leadership class fully devoted to their own economic success, which means they will almost inevitably want to be sexually active in their twenties without the burden of procreation (enjoying the fornicator's desire for the unitive good separated from the procreative good) and willing to outsource child-raising and the formation of their children's souls to the state and those it certifies as day care workers and public school teachers (separating the procreative good from the life of their own household). This is an ideal of success that we will have to learn to reject, I think, if we are to understand the virtue of chastity and teach our own children to see the connection between chastity and the wealth of life.

2

Practicing Christianity in the Age of Technology

Donna Freitas

LATELY, I AM WORRIED about our humanity.

 Basic things about it: our sense of self on a fundamental level; our capacity to see; our *willingness* to see. Our desire to look at the world, at those around us, in all of our delight and pain, this desire as though a commandment from God. I am concerned about self-awareness, our self-consciousness about our own behaviors, the importance of coming to consciousness about ourselves, the possibility that we are abandoning such efforts, such human and spiritual quests, without even realizing what we are giving up, or that we are giving these things up. I wonder what role faith, religions in general, might hold in helping us to reclaim these things, helping us to remember or perhaps, to realize for the first time, why these aspects of our selves, our lives, our humanity are fundamental to not only our own well-being, but to the well-being of all people, children, citizens of this world. I worry that we are letting go of the task of interiority, the cultivation of it, as much as we are ignoring exteriority, and the cultivation of it, too.

 These questions and concerns have arisen prior to but also certainly because of my most recent work about social media, smartphones, and young adulthood, for which I conducted a national study across thirteen colleges and universities in the United States, Catholic, evangelical, private-secular and public institutions among them.

The First Crossroad and How Christianity Failed Today's Young Adults

Before I discuss this research more directly, I want to remark, first, on the role of religion—or the *problem* of religion in relation to my other work—which has formed the bulk of my scholarly endeavors for well over a decade, about sex on campus, about sex and young adulthood and all that it implies (including #MeToo related topics, Title IX, etc.). Here, more than anything else, religion has been an obstacle rather than a boon within my conversations with college students and that research.

Most young adults see the teachings of religions around sex and gender as intolerant, sexist, impossible, and, in certain cases, hateful. Most religious traditions, especially the Christian traditions, have chosen to come down on prohibitions around sex, gender, and sexual orientation, as their focus, especially in relation to young adults. Rather than give young adults spiritual tools and skills for discernment and wise decision-making around sex in their lives, religions mainly choose to pass on a set of don'ts, which most young adults likewise discard angrily. These don'ts communicate a refusal to them by these traditions—a refusal to listen, to see, to hear, to want to know the lives of young adults today and all the difficult, complicated choices they face as sexual beings in this particular moment in our history. Religions, in particular the Christian traditions, seem to prefer to leave young adults swimming on their own in a vast sea.[1]

---

1. I have written extensively on religions and, in particular, Christianity and Catholicism in relation to young adults and sex. For a selection of these writings, please see the following books: Donna Freitas, *Sex and the Soul (Updated Edition): Juggling Sexuality, Spirituality, Romance and Religion on America's College Campuses* (New York: Oxford University Press, 2015); Donna Freitas, *Consent on Campus: A Manifesto* (New York: Oxford University Press, 2018); and please also see the following articles: Donna Freitas, "Sex and the Single Student Today, an Interview with Donna Freitas," *Conversations on Jesuit Higher Education* 37.1 (2010) art. 7 (this article can be read at https://epublications.marquette.edu/conversations/vol37/iss1/7); Donna Freitas "Consent and the Catholic University: Social Justice and Sexuality," *Conversations on Jesuit Higher Education* 51.1 (2017) art. 17 (this article can be read at https://epublications.marquette.edu/conversations/vol51/iss1/17).

When I make such claims in front of Christian theologians, I am often met with loud and fervent protests that this is such an impoverished take on Catholicism's (for example) understanding of sex in relation to our humanity and its role in our lives—which I understand, but only to a point. The Christian traditions, and Catholicism in particular, certainly are—or, *could* be, *should* be—able to offer more than a series of don'ts. However, while this "more" might be evident to a theologian, it is *not* so obvious on the ground for your average Catholic young adult. All that trickles down are the don'ts, because your average Catholic does not have a PhD in theology. They hear the uproar about the presence of condoms on campus, and worse still, the similar uproar about all things regarding LGBTQ issues, and they know all about the abuse scandal and how utterly overwhelmingly enormous and horrific it is, and the moral authority of any member of the Catholic hierarchy on the issue of sex just vanishes. (As it should. This tradition has behaved badly, terribly, reprehensibly, especially with respect to children, and so have other Christian denominations as we have been learning in the press of late.[2]) And so—unless you are one of the rare, conservative, party-line Catholic young adults who belong to your college's chapter of the Love & Fidelity Network—on the topic of sex and all that goes with it, Catholicism has basically nothing to say to you.

But worse still than this perception among young adults and college students in particular, this generation believes that the people in power in Christianity—rather than try to see, to listen, to hear, to witness what young adults live today—have turned their backs, have deafened themselves, have shouted in favor of orthodoxy, have screamed really, so loudly that this screaming has drowned out the voices and needs and woundedness of an entire generation. Christianity has failed at the task of Good Samaritanism on the issue of sex and #MeToo. Rather than

---

2. The list of articles surrounding the sex abuse scandal could fill an entire book, but one particularly upsetting one (in my opinion) was reported more recently. Please see Laurie Goodstein and Sharon Otterman, "Catholic Priests Abused 1000 Children in Pennsylvania, Report Says," *The New York Times* (April 14, 2018), https://nyti.ms/2MKE086. With respect to the growing scandals amid other Christian churches and denominations, see also Elizabeth Dias, "Her Evangelical Megachurch Was Her World. Then Her Daughter Said She was Molested by a Minister," *The New York Times* (June 10, 2019), https://nyti.ms/2IwQSPJ; and see also *The Houston Chronicle* and *San Antonio Express-News* joint, in depth, multi-part investigative series on sex abuse within the Southern Baptist Church: "Abuse of Faith," https://www.houstonchronicle.com/local/investigations/abuse-of-faith/.

choose to *see*, really *see*, the dilemmas, choices, and challenges today's young adults face, to try and respect where they are, and their unique circumstances, rather than being a tradition of tolerance, openness, and love, this tradition and the hierarchy along with it have walked arrogantly by as young adults lie, broken and alone, on the side of the road.

The reason I set this problem out, about sex and this generation, is that I think the world's religions and Christianity in particular face another urgent, contemporary dilemma with respect to new technologies—in particular, social media and our ever-present smartphones. My hope is that we will choose wisely this time—and with a kind of engaged, self-awareness and sense of practicality—as we figure out what this tradition can offer humanity that has relevance *on the ground*. I believe we still have choices ahead of us, and the first step is to recognize that we do. My reflections here are an effort toward that end.

I'll also say at the start that, unlike the extraordinary challenges and negativity swirling around the topic of sex and Christianity, sex and religion, which provokes disdain from so many young adults today, on the issue of new technologies, religions including Christianity are in a very different position. I see people turning toward Christianity, looking toward it for help, for answers, for new understanding, for sheer and basic *health* and well-being in this area of their life. I want to address what Christian spirituality and the Catholic social justice tradition might offer this conversation. And I want to emphasize how, because of social media and smartphones, the world's religions, including Christianity, are at another crossroads with this generation of young adults.

Let's not fail this time.

Using Our Devices vs. Being Used by Them

On the subject of technology, I would like to paint a brief portrait of some of the main issues and struggles young adults face today (which are also very similar, often identical, to the issues that all people face because of new technology, in particular smartphones and all that go with them).[3]

I want to start with the smartphone, and the way it has changed our lives. There are many things that it offers us—GPS, easy communication

---

3. For a full overview of the findings from my research, please see Donna Freitas, *The Happiness Effect: How Social Media Is Driving a Generation to Appear Perfect at Any Cost* (New York: Oxford University Press, 2017).

for logistics, Uber. It has also become the primary social media delivery device, whether Facebook, Instagram, or Snapchat is your preference. It makes our lives "easy"—but it also has made them incredibly difficult. We now know that apps and the phone itself are expressly designed to addict us (see Tristan Harris and his Center for Humane Technology[4]), to hold us in their thrall much like a vampire. One of the questions we need to ask ourselves then is: What does social media suck from us? What is the life force inside us that diminishes as we hold our phones in our palms? And, of course, how do we right this imbalance? How do we take it back?

One of the big questions of the digital age is this: what does it mean to have a healthy relationship with our devices? And related: what does a healthy relationship look like? Is it the same or different for everyone? Is it possible that there is no such thing as a healthy relationship for some people?

The students I interviewed for my study about social media, smartphones, and the college experience said many things, but fundamental to all of them were a few core struggles. The first had to do with stress and pressure. Social media has taught this generation to "brand" themselves, that it is imperative to be careful of their own personal "brand," and that the stakes of posting are enormously high; one ill-advised or ill-phrased post or photo can ruin a person's life, close the door (permanently) to getting into college, and/or close the door to getting a job. Anything one discloses—political leanings, religious leanings, what one does socially and who one hangs out with (or doesn't) can have a negative impact on one's future. It doesn't matter that all young adults know that everyone lies online, that social media is "fake" (a problem that almost all students spoke of during the interview process, and long before the election and everyone bemoaning "fake news" in this country). Social media still has the power to (potentially) ruin your life and your future.

Alongside potential professional consequences are the social struggles that social media sets up for young adults. Key among these, my interviewee Emma explained, is that going online every day, all the time, is terrible for a person's self-esteem. It is always "the worst version" of herself vs. the "best version of everyone else," as Emma put it. Many, *many* students expressed some version of what Emma described, and how this experience of feeling bad about oneself, lonely, left out, overlooked, less successful, less popular than *everyone else*, has become a regular feature

---

4. See their website at https://humanetech.com.

of their daily lives, and the smartphone is the preferred delivery device of this particular contemporary affliction.

During the study, students did express love for their smartphones. There were students who *named* their phones (affectionately so), students who described the relationship in Lady Gaga–esque terminology (like a bad romance) and students who likened leaving the house without their smartphone as though going out "without [their] heart or [their] brain" (in the words of one young man). Of the students who participated in the online survey, 69 percent described feeling that, because of smartphones, our society (and parents, teachers, coaches, etc. along with it) have set the expectation that young adults (or really, all of us) must live as though "on call" twenty-four-seven, as though we are doctors and surgeons, "on" and "immediately available" both day and night—even while we are sleeping, many students emphasized.

And, as with Emma, one of the themes that arose again and again among interviewees was the sense, the *knowledge*, that while students knew they should be—that they *want* to be—users of social media and smartphones, their reality is something quite different. As much as students love their smartphones, the vast majority also feel *used* by social media and by these devices. Because of this, they love them, but they also resent them. They feel compelled, helpless, unable to turn away even if it makes them feel bad—addicted, in other words. Students spoke of an ongoing struggle to right this problem, to go from "being used" to becoming a "us*er*," someone in control of it, as opposed to being controlled by it. It is a battle that never ends, fought in fits and starts, a charger left home on purpose, a camping trip where phones are not allowed, a parent who takes the phone away and provokes a revelation/remembrance of how good life can be without it—amazing really. But then the phone is recharged, the camping trip is over, the parent gives the phone back, and all is reset and the battle ahead once again.

So, though the smartphone can offer us so much, right now our relationship to it is one of terrific imbalance. This lack of balance is costly.

But I also believe that if we can right this imbalance, maybe this device could be what it should be: something of great and convenient use to us. I want us to become self-aware of the possible costs of this device to us, so we can make informed choices about it. I want us to become critical thinkers about our devices, because it is only with critical thinking that we can shift things in a positive direction. And this place—this area of power imbalance, of feeling used, controlled, compelled, helpless—is the place I want to focus our attention, and where I believe that Christianity has quite a lot to offer our world, if only we can put it expressly toward that end.

The focus to which I'd like to turn our attention, right now, is exactly this—*attention*. Our ability to attend to the world and each other is something that our devices endanger. In the process, they endanger one of the very core aspects of our humanity.

The Problem of Attention

In the fall semester of 2018, I taught a series of readings to my students that were designed to get them to think about their relationship to the world, and the attention they pay to it (or lack thereof) in light of new technology. Thoreau's *Walden*, chapter 2, "Where I Lived and What I Lived For"; E. B. White's *Charlotte's Web*; Emily Dickinson's poetry; and Dodie Smith's *I Capture the Castle* all made the list, and all of which—*I* think—interrupt our contemporary lives with people, characters, and thinking that is particularly attentive to nature, the world, and everyone in it. Thoreau seems to speak to the stresses and challenges of our day from well over a hundred years ago, about the frantic pace of life, about living as though zombies, about what it means to step back from the busy-ness of the world. I challenged my students to think of unplugging from their smartphones and Wi-Fi as their very own "metaphorical cabin in the woods," which to them could involve an hour, an afternoon, even a day away. We talked about E. B. White's love for the natural world and his willingness to become fascinated by even the smallest of creatures—as small and as still as a spider sac, one that would become the inspiration for one of the greatest children's books of all time, a book that speaks of love and friendship and justice as the most important things we can all embody in this life. And so on and so forth.

In the course of our discussions, my students spoke of reading—of *how* they read. One student started by saying that she doesn't—she *can't*—read more than one sentence at a time. She reads one sentence, then looks at her phone, then reads another sentence, then looks at her phone again. This provoked a conversation among my class about how hard it is to read more than one sentence at a time, or write more than one sentence at time. Their discussion became a conversation about *attention*, about how impossible it is to give one's attention in any sustained way, how our smartphones make sustained attention, focus, concentration, nearly impossible in the lives of today's college students, or at least, the ones in that class.

Because of my research about college students, I am often asked why there is so much anxiety and depression among students today. Is it because of hookup culture? Is it because of social media?

After this conversation with my own students, I could not stop thinking of something far more basic at the root of this issue—the simple ability to focus. To concentrate. Our ability to attend to something, just one thing, for more than thirty seconds. The pleasures that can be found in such focus (think Csikszentmihalyi's ideas about *flow*, a kind of altered state that occurs when one's attention is wholly captured by an activity, or some sort of experience, a sight, a place[5]). So much creativity, so much joy, can come for our ability to, our *willingness* to watch, to look, from our desire to see. Just imagine the fragmentation of self, of time, of learning, of reading, if one literally feels so compelled by an object—not a positive object (not a tiny spider sac that captured E. B. White and inspired a masterpiece, or maybe a bee as with Emily Dickinson's beautiful, playful poetry) but a *smartphone*, an object that makes so many of us feel *helpless in the face of it*—that makes my students feel they literally cannot turn away from this thing for more than thirty seconds.

An inability to *attend* not only makes it impossible to get required things done (homework, the paper that is due, that test one needs to study for), but the leisure of enjoying something *other than a smartphone* is also lost. An engrossing novel on a rainy afternoon, an engrossing task enjoyed, an engrossing person with whom we are conversing. Lost, too, is the gift of self-knowledge that comes from allowing ourselves to be so wholly captured by an art form, an extraordinary sight of natural wonder, another living being. Lost to us is the experienced of becoming, of *being* wholly other-centered.

Other-centered. Self-emptying.

What we become when we attend to the world and those around us.

The giving over of attention can have the creative effect of building up another person, of anchoring them to the world, of communicating to that person, *You matter, because* this *matters, this connection we have made*. In the process it anchors us, it builds us, it communicates to us that we matter, too, that we are connected, too. And this is the place where I

---

5. See Mihaly Csikszentmihalyi, *Flow: The Psychology of Optimal Experience* (New York: Harper & Row, 1990).

believe that the Christian tradition, and in particular Simone Weil, has so much to say to our current predicament, and this next generation who is growing up in the middle of such tremendous struggle.

Simone Weil to the Rescue

For Simone Weil, our willingness to look, to see, to *pay attention* is the beginning of the end of suffering in this world. Attention, looking, seeing is the cornerstone of social justice. The willingness to allow oneself to be wholly captured by the presence of another person, their joy, their pain, their delight, their woundedness, is powerful—so powerful that for Weil, it is grace itself.

"Not only does the love of God have attention for its substance," writes Weil,

> the love of our neighbor, which we know to be the same love, is made of this same substance. Those who are happy have no need for anything in this world but people capable of giving them their attention. The capacity to give one's attention to a sufferer is a very rare and difficult thing; it is almost a miracle; it *is* a miracle. . . . The love of our neighbor in all its fullness simply means being able to say to him: "What are you going through?" It is a recognition that the sufferer exists, not only as a unit in a collection, or a specimen from the social category labeled "unfortunate," but as a man, exactly like we are, who was one day stamped with a special mark by affliction. For this reason it is enough, but it is indispensable, to know how to look at him in a certain way.[6]

For Weil, the mere willingness to look upon someone who is suffering has the power to restore their humanity; it is creative in this regard. "Happy then are those who pass their adolescence and youth in developing this power of attention," she writes. "Whoever goes through years of study without developing this attention within himself has lost a great treasure."[7] Attention is a spiritual practice in and of itself, a practice with transformative power—for both other and self. "The soul empties itself of all its own contents in order to receive into itself the being it is looking at," Weil says, "just as he is, in all his truth. Only he who is capable of

---

6. Simone Weil, *Waiting on God*, Routledge Revivals (New York: Routledge, 2009), 36.

7. Weil, *Waiting on God*, 36.

attention can do this."[8] For Weil, to be a Good Samaritan, *is to be willing to see* the suffering person on the side of the road. That act of seeing is the beginning of our humanity—by one human turning to and seeing the woundedness of another, we hold the power to restore the humanity of that other, and in the process, restore our own humanity, too.

And yet, we are now living in a world and during a time—this digital age—when attention, the basic willingness to look each other in the eye, or even given one another a passing glance, has become a rarity. When I walk around New York City, when I am on the subway or waiting in line at a coffee shop, I sometimes try and count the people who are *not* engrossed in their phones. I do this, too, when I am on the campus where I teach. Nearly half the people are staring at their phones on the streets and the trains and even more of the students at my university are doing the same as they go from class to class. Rather than talking to each other when I walk in the door of my classroom, most of my students are silent, staring down at their phones on their desks.

For Weil, the kind of attention she is talking about—the kind that is grace—is *intentional*. It must be learned, it must be prioritized, its value must be grasped.

But right now, in our world, even the most *basic* kinds of attending to others, the unpracticed sort, the kind that is simply people looking at other people as they wander the world, is being left by the wayside. This most basic form of respect—sheer acknowledgment of each other's existence—is no longer a given.

And yet what if, in light of Simone Weil, the act of looking—in our case, *looking up* from our phones—is the most basic form of social justice we might practice? And because of those phones, we are absolutely out of practice of doing this? Is *looking down* at these screens, the newest, most common form of vice, the kind of practiced vice that Aristotle might warn against? And what if the cost of our failure to look, our *unwillingness* to look, and the fact that our desire to look has been *wrested away* by devices designed, is not only the kind of creative attention of which Weil speaks, but is at the same time the creative attention *due to ourselves*? Interiority, the development of an interior life, the ability to focus, to *attend*, is central to becoming a person, to our own humanity, to self-discovery in all of our gifts and talents, ideas and passions. Attention is both paid outward and paid inward, and today we neglect both of its directions.

---

8. Weil, *Waiting on God*, 36.

Attention in and of itself is a good, it is worthwhile, it is a virtue. It is constitutive of both self and other, it is the backbone of relationship, of meaningful existence, and yet it is becoming such a rare commodity, especially in its undivided form. It is true that our devices demand our undivided attention and yet at the same time divide that attention, fragment it, explode it into tiny pieces so as to render it meaningless, empty—turning the good, the virtue that attention is, that it is meant to be, into a vice that plagues us. So, the divided, corrupted attention that we experience on our devices, replaces the good, the *grace*-full attention that Weil longs for us to practice.

If the body, as understood by medieval mystics like Teresa of Avila and friends, was the obstacle to the soul and therefore to God, the smartphone is now the obstacle to the body and all else.

In *The Interior Castle*, Teresa of Avila presents a kind of training for the battle between soul and body—a battle for the soul, for the interior life, toward the end of reaching God, that must fight the body's passions and desires lest they eclipse the more patient, quieter, more divine aspects of ourselves, the more lovely qualities of the soul that we might miss altogether because of the body's drumbeat. Today, we need to undergo a similar sort of training, so as not to miss the body itself, the body, the mind, the soul, the heart, and the way all of these aspects of our humanity together can play in concert toward the end of human connection, love, citizenship, toward the end of social justice, toward the end of humanity itself.

The New Crossroad: Christian Spirituality and All It Offers the Digital Age

The wonderful thing about spiritual practices is that they are just this: practices. Things you practice, that you try on, that you work toward incorporating into your life. Attention—the kind of which Weil speaks—is a spiritual practice that must be learned like all others, and today we are in dire need of learning it. I believe our very selves depend on it, and the promotion of justice within this world depends on it. The practice that is attention (and attention which, for Weil and so many Christian mystics, is a form of prayer), is not only essential for the spiritual life but for life at all, for us to become human and to practice our humanity among others.

To come back to one of my primary questions: how can the spiritual practices of the Christian tradition serve to promote digital health and well-being? How can they help us to become *users* of our devices, rather than *feeling* or *being used* by them?

By helping this generation (and all of us) take these longtime spiritual practices and traditions and show us how these practices can interrupt the digital era in ways that help us hold onto our humanity, and in ways that help us to develop an interior life that is reciprocal with an exterior life that has an eye toward justice. By teaching us how these practices are empowering and transformative *right in that very place* where so many of us feel totally and utterly helpless (i.e., in the face of our smartphones). By helping us learn to stay where we are, to see inside ourselves, to see outside ourselves, to direct our attention toward the things and people who make us more human, not less. To live a meaningful life despite and in spite of these devices which, yes, can be convenient, but which also get in the way of us becoming the best of who we are meant to be.

3

"Struck Down, but not Destroyed . . ."

Paul R. Hinlicky

"Like a bolt out of the blue," the neurologist said to me, stricken as I lay in the intensive care unit at Union Memorial Hospital in Baltimore. "That's why we call it a stroke." Suddenly "struck down" in this respect, similar to what befell Saul on the road to Damascus: unanticipated and without forewarning. But a connection of that Paul who became the apostle of the crucified but risen One with this Paul, latter-day Lutheran theologian, is more than fortuitous. How often I appropriated the apostle to the nations in those trying moments! I held onto especially a snippet from my ordination sermon text from many years before, full-well-knowing at the same time the dissimilarity between Paul's sense in it as one persecuted from without and my own appropriation of it as one injured from within: "struck down but not destroyed."

Having said goodbyes to attendees of the annual theological conference of the Center for Catholic and Evangelical Theology (of which I am a board member) and a group of students from Roanoke College who had accompanied me, we were descending the staircase from the fourth-story conference on our way to the board meeting of the Center. Construction was going on outside with a huge concrete pumping machine at work; I turned back to look at the technological marvel through the glass walls and collapsed on the staircase. Dazed, I was helped to my feet. I thought I had missed my step, fallen and struck my jaw on the handrail.

I stammered that I thought I'd gotten a concussion. Unbelievably in hindsight, I walked all the way down the staircase until those around me forced me to sit down. Through the fog I perceived all of them looking concerned at my appearance. I distinctly recall Carl Braaten giving the order to call an ambulance. As the ambulance sped me to the stroke unit at Union Memorial, the medic attending me said, "I hate to tell you this, buddy, but I think you're having a stroke."

Cognitive dissonance—another resemblance to Paul knocked off his high horse on the road to Damascus: what could it mean that the crucified blasphemer whose spreading cult he was determined to arrest now appeared to him in glory identifying, as his own body, those whom Paul was persecuting?

My dissonance was in this respect similar. Three weeks before, I had been in the Canadian Rockies for a theological conference. On an afternoon off, I hiked with some of my hosts five steep uphill miles to view spectacular waterfalls. Healthy as a horse was I! What on earth had just happened to me? "Perplexed, but not forsaken"—another echo of 2 Corinthians 4 came to me. If you have to have a stroke, it couldn't have happened to me at a better time and place or with better company. In my confusion I may have forgotten some, but I particularly remember the special care given to me, and on behalf of me to my distraught loved ones, by Michael Root, Jim Buckley, Dwight Penas, and Gregory and Carol Fryer. I was not forsaken.

But I was perplexed. What's the good of humanity? That's the theological question which this volume addresses. What's the good of one individual human life? That is an existential version of our question which pressed hard upon my muddled mind in those first forty-eight hours when I was on neurosurgical watch, awakened regularly and interrogated to the point of exasperation as they monitored the function of my damaged brain. What good am I—now? An existential version of that more essentialist formulation about the good in general of humanity in general is especially fitting, I suppose, for a Lutheran theologian to meditate on.

It may be a manifestation of a streak of recklessness in my character and it may also be just the deep tranquility of faith—I still can't tell the difference in myself—but I can honestly say that throughout the ordeal I had no fear of death for my own sake. Rather my thoughts went immediately to the suffering my untimely death would cause my loved ones, especially my adult son. If I am still in some respects a Lutheran existentialist, it is as coupled with the communitarian ontology of the Beloved Community, as the latter is represented but also regularly betrayed by the—if, damning with faint praise, I may retool Leonid Brezhnev's notorious defense of Soviet communism—betrayed by the "real existing" church. In any case, already in the ambulance, the prayer that flitted heavenward from my bewildered mind was that the Lord would spare my little life because my death at this juncture would be just too cruel for my son.

Raised in a loving and adventurous family, maturing with strapping good looks and an acute mind filled with curiosity, his difficulty launching in his twenties baffled Ellen and me. It was only after he had moved back in with us a few years before my stroke that the depth of his suffering became apparent and that we were able finally to get a proper diagnosis of his mental distress. In breaking through to that painful discovery, he and I had grown very close. He had felt forsaken so much in life, also by God, and consequently so drained of trust, that my renewed presence in his life in these difficult years built a bridge to which he could cling. For his sake, I could not now die. So that was my prayer, as befogged but earnest I, to use a colorful expression of Martin Luther, "rubbed God's ears in his promises."

As I have reflected in these two years on the spontaneous prayer I offered up in this dire moment, I have realized that it also implied a belief about myself: as I have lived my life believing, in Bonhoeffer's words, that Jesus "is the man for others," so at this very moment, not knowing what good I would be for anything else, I somehow believed that I would still be good for another.

I spent a week at Union Memorial Hospital which was also for me a study in contrasts between the excellent medical care that I received as a well-insured person on the one side and the striking class, gender, and race divisions visible both in the ranks of those who served me and in those treated alongside of me. Is the good of my individual life little more than my privileged capacity to pay for it? Why shouldn't this excellent care be available to any and all?

A previous church generation called Jesus our Great Physician, healer of soul and body. The present generation has learned with some success that ministry in Jesus' name cannot truthfully lay claim to the soul while leaving the body to the devil. The ministry of the reign of God which Jesus inaugurates when he comes into Galilee—notice the present tense with which I express this—is a work of healing: faith and forgiveness for the guilty and despairing soul, but also sight for the blind, mental freedom from the tyranny of unclean spirits, food for the hungry. The apocalyptic framework of the Gospels tells us that these works of healing by Jesus were at once assaults on the devil's tyranny and foretastes of the promised resurrection.

Aye, there's the rub, if I may now speak to fellow ministers of the gospel. Healing, however real, is temporary; only the resurrection is everlasting. Pastors and priests who engage ministries of healing with their communities of faith wrestle daily with this evanescence of healing, if I may put it this way, what scholars call the "eschatological reservation."

Healed, finished, done with, mission accomplished, time to move on! Wouldn't that be great? But the faithful and persevering minister of the gospel knows better. As we are to be satisfied with daily bread so must we also be satisfied with daily healing. The minister of the gospel is the one who keeps on keeping on, daily pulling body and soul from the pits into which they have fallen, knowing full well that tomorrow they may fall again. Here successes are temporary because they are and can only be real as foretastes of something yet to come. Thus the pastoral faith which ministers healing care is often on trial precisely because until the kingdom comes in power and glory it is deprived of a final resolution. Pauline perplexity at being struck down but not destroyed thus remains the marching order for a church militant. For the Christian this life is becoming not being, labor not rest, healing not wholeness. It is not by accident that in the great eighth chapter of Romans Paul insists that we with all creation need yet await in eager longing "the redemption of our bodies."

But there's also a gift of clarity in the midst of this perplexity if only we can faithfully abide in it. What humanity has in common is not a state of consciousness but a state of bodily-ness. It is the state of bodily-ness that is foundational in that it connects human beings to one another and to the good earth and only so also to God our common creator and redeemer and fulfiller. The ontology of beloved community is thus existentially to be discovered in the bodily reality of creation; this comes as a discovery, however, because the bodily reality of creation is distorted and obscured from sight by our uniquely human apostasy, which is the bone-deep despair of unbelief.

Freed from sorrow, freed from sin, creation's hope for the victory of beloved community emerges afresh for perception and participation as the earthly body of the risen Lord comes on the scene and thus appears in the midst of our brokenness. As the risen Lord Jesus identified himself to Paul on the road to Damascus with those whom Paul persecuted, so

Paul realized that body is no arbitrary metaphor for the community of gospel faith: the risen Lord really has an earthly body composed of his called people, an *ecclesia*. Precisely as such a real body on the earth, the ecclesia can be wounded from without, but also as subsequent Christian history teaches, injured from within. There's the rub. Just as profoundly engaged in the world's hurting and hurtful messiness, the body of Christ too becomes wounded from within, riven by sinful divisions, broken into rival factions. The ministry of healing thus comes to define not only the ministry of the church to the world but also applies, indeed urgently, to the wounded church. We must intentionally be *pro ecclesia*. A fractured body of Christ cannot heal in the world as it ought as it is itself in need of healing.

So I have seen this time of trial in my little life as a microcosm of the state of the church today: struck down but not destroyed, perplexed but not forsaken. Whether we say with Thomas Aquinas that doing follows from being or with Martin Luther that the work follows from the person, in either case we are pointed thereby to the maimed body of Christ which we have in common, in need of healing from within. That ecumenical ministry of healing has been the mission of the Center for Catholic and Evangelical Theology, just as in our own pastoral ministries and communities of faith we are about the healing of hurting bodies and sorrowing souls around us.

4

Male and Female, the Image of God, and the Significance of Children

Edith M. Humphrey

CHRISTIANS ARE QUITE ACCUSTOMED to speaking about the Holy Trinity as a mystery. God's triune nature presents us with a paradox so obvious that we recognize the difficulty of describing it, and so theologians, liturgists and the creeds use multiple metaphors, *caveats*, and boundaries. In trying to grasp and to pass on this mystery, we follow in the tradition of the Hebrews, Israelites, and ancient Jews, who hesitated even to name God, and whose visionary literature was hedged around with warnings and signals of approximation, such as the words "like" and "appearance" (e.g., Ezek 1:28). As Christians, of course, we know that the Father has, for the sake of the Son, called us "friends" and made us into his real children: we have been let in on what prophets and righteous ones longed to see (cf. Matt 13:17). Moreover, we know that the Holy Spirit has come among us, teaching us from the least to the greatest (Heb 8:11). Still, the mystery of the One who is God remains, and the faithful Christian will approach the burning bush with great care.

It is not so apparent that a human being, and humanity together, is likewise a great mystery. We should not be surprised, however, that this is so. Two conjoined tenets of Judaism at the time of Jesus—a holy God, and a holy people—were maintained steadfastly by the renewed people of God, his church.¹ If we share in God's holiness, then it is not unlikely that we also will partake in his characteristic of mystery. This probably was more obvious to early Christians than it is to some of us today, who think individualistically about the faith. The popularity of a book like *The Shepherd of Hermas* in the second century testifies to this ancient perception of our corporate nature. In this book's first four visions, Lady Church appears astonishingly in three human forms, each progressively more vigorous, and also as a temple in the process of being built by God and his angels. While many apocalypses focus upon mysteries in the heavens or in the future, *The Shepherd* concentrates upon a present, yet ongoing mystery: the church herself. We see a similar appreciation of the mystery of the church in the New Testament Apocalypse, where she is pictured as a glorious but persecuted woman (Rev 12) and as the New Jerusalem (Rev 21–22), coming from God as a habitation for all who trust in him.

In this essay, I will attempt to recover something of the wonder with which the historic church approached our humanity, made in the image of God, and recreated for his glory. We will explore the mystery of our composite human nature, set out some boundaries for talking about this mystery (both in itself and in relation to God), and consider the deep significance of children as an integral part of being human.² Finally, I will close by examining the "hard cases" of celibacy and childlessness, and why Christians think of these states (and should continue to think of them) as holding great value.

I. Humanity, the Sacramentality of Creation, and the New Creation

The composite nature of mysterious humanity is registered in the New Testament and in various patristic pieces, where these works speak of the relation between husband and wife. The first book of the Bible describes

---

1. For an exploration of these two tenets among the four "pillars" of Second Temple Judaism, see James J. D. Dunn, *The Partings of the Ways: Between Christianity and Judaism and their Significance for the Character of Christianity* (London: SCM Press, 1991), 18–36.

2. An earlier and briefer version of the first two elements of this paper was presented at Holy Trinity Monastery/Seminary (Jordanville), during the conference held on May 7–9, 2019, entitled "Chastity, Purity, Integrity: Orthodox Anthropology and Secular Culture in the 21st Century." Its proceedings will be published by HTM/HTS Press.

both Adam, the first human being, and the couple, Adam and Eve, as created after the very image of God. In case the use of contemporary versions has obscured the mystery for us, let us be reminded of the interplay between unity and duality in that great deliberative statement, and action of God:

> "Let us make *man* [Adam] in our image, after our likeness, and let *them* have dominion" . . . So God created man [Adam] in His own image, in the image of God He created *him*; male and female He created *them*. (Gen 1:26–27)[3]

The tension here is harder to grasp in contemporary English, so I have left "Adam" intact. Alas, we do not have a word accepted by all today that can mean both an individual and the group, as "Man" once served us: this is an impoverishment, in my view! But the complex play back and forth between singular and plural, "him" and "them," unity and duality, makes it clear that, both together and singly, the original humans shared in God's image, and in God's rule over the rest of creation (Gen 1:28). This sense of mystery and specific care for the human creation is continued in the particular actions taken by the LORD in the story of Genesis 2: He breathes into Adam the breath of life; he specifically separates Eve as a partner for him; and he calls this apex of his creating activity "very good."

Ephesians 5, despite its practical exigencies, breathes a similar air of astonishment. The ideal male and female, bound together in Christ, are to be in mutual submission ("be subject one to the other out of reverence for Christ" [Eph 5:21]) yet their relationship is not wholly symmetrical. The wife especially is to show respect, while the husband is to show sacrifice—and together, Paul (or his disciple) declares they show forth "the mystery of Christ and the Church." Here the letter fills out the tantalizing image that the apostle uses when speaking of his hopes for the Corinthians, that he might finally offer them, in fulfillment of their espousal to the LORD, as a "pure virgin" (2 Cor 11:2).

Finally, in the final pages of the Bible, we view with fascination and yearning the descent and *début* of the fruitful New Jerusalem, prepared as a bride adorned for her husband, and calling out, with the Holy Spirit and the visionary John, "Even so, come, Lord Jesus!" (Rev 22:17–20). The metaphor of bride and bridegroom, then, is considered so poignant and appropriate that it brings our holy canon to its conclusion.

---

3. Translations of the scriptural passages are my own.

From one perspective, this effusive language about husband and wife may strike us as very odd. After all, though we are created in the image of God, surely our sexuality, of all things, is something that we share with the animals. To the animals, as well as to the first human couple, God said, "Be fruitful and multiply." As C. S. Lewis once put it, our status as human beings is "amphibious," living as a whole being, both in the flesh and in the spirit. If some have adopted a "partitive" view of our humanity (flesh as one part, spirit as another), and James Dunn has preferred an "aspective" view,[4] we may add to these a third way of considering our state: the *contextual*, that is, *where* we dwell. However we understand our complexity, we might assume that surely our sexuality is part of the fleshly aspect, or context, rather than the spiritual. The common wisdom is that we are linked with the animal world in our embodied and gendered condition, but with God in our rationality, our will, our capacity to love, and so on.

However, this assumption says more about our tendency to subtle dualism than it does about the Christian view of humanity, or the biblical texts and traditions that engender our understanding. When the beginning, middle, and end of Scriptures suggest that our gendered being is connected with cosmic mystery, and when this is a tradition carried on by the church in her hymnody and prayers, then we need to take heed. And this is even more critical in our day when the concept of human sexuality and gender has been subjected first to scientific rationalization, and then described in terms of mere enculturation and subjective preference. A very clear and destructive challenge to dominical teaching is the presumption that Jesus was simply bound by his culture when he declared, "From the beginning . . . God created them male and female" (Mark 10:6).

Instead, our Christian story, beginning with Genesis, has viewed the creation of humanity, male and female, as both a good in itself and as an ineffable mystery which joins us both with the created order and to the holy God. The swiftness with which the text moves from "after our image" to "male and female" in Genesis 1:27 suggests an *amplifying* parallelism: somehow our maleness and femaleness is part of our image-bearing. In harmony with this, the stories of the patriarchs emphasize

---

4. James D. G. Dunn, *The Theology of Paul the Apostle* (Grand Rapids: Eerdmans, 1998), 54. His ideas have been incorporated by Nancey Murphy, in both the essay printed in this volume and also in "Do Humans Have Souls? Perspectives from Philosophy, Science, and Religion," *Interpretation* 67.1 (2013) 30–41, esp. 33.

Abraham *and* Sarah, Isaac *and* Rebecca, Jacob *and* Rachel (and, as a complication, Leah). Among other great metaphors, the image of the passionate Husband-God and his wife, Israel (frequently pictured as wayward), grows strong in the Old Testament, in the books of Hosea, Jeremiah, and Isaiah, and in the traditional reading of the Song of Solomon. This ability of the husband-wife relationship (with its concomitant family) to point beyond itself persists, even while the *natural* goodness of marriage is also celebrated throughout the Scriptures.

We might remark here that the significance of marriage (with the familial state) as a natural good has been muted somewhat in Protestant traditions because of the marginalization of the "extra" books and stories named variously by our communities as deuterocanonical, readable, or apocryphal. We may think of the major theme of the book of Tobit—Tobias's fidelity and God-honored marriage to Rachel—or of the poignant bridal language used to describe Wisdom's alliance with the faithful in Sirach, or the steadfastness of the Maccabean mother (traditionally called "Solomonia"[5]) with her sons in the face of tyranny.

Such books were dismissed by the Reformers not only because of the presence of awkward proof-texts in the Roman-Protestant debates about merit and grace, but also, it would seem, because some of the narratives appeared all-too-human, and too trivial to retain a place among books with more exalted themes. However, the presence of such stories in the collection of Holy Writ, I would suggest, prepared the imagination of God's people to understand husband and wife (with the family) as a *sacramental reality*: something good in itself, but that directs us beyond the human good to a deeper mystery. Saint Irenaeus, in speaking about "the glory of God" as "living human being," explained that "the manifestation of God . . . is made by means of the creation."[6] In saying this, he argued that even the created order reveals God, and brings spiritual life. In our own day, the beloved Fr. Alexander Schmemann has spoken of "the world" which "becomes an epiphany of God, a source of his revelation, presence, and power," in the creatures of bread, wine, water and oil, for

---

5. This is the traditional name of the mother of the seven martyrs in 2 Maccabees 7 and 4 Maccabees 1–17, as given by the Eastern Church. She is celebrated in the church not only for her fidelity and courage, but also as a prophetess who proclaimed clearly the doctrine of *creatio ex nihilo* (2 Macc 7:28), followed by Saint Paul in Romans 4:17 and by the author of the epistle to the Hebrews (11:3).

6. Irenaeus, *Haer.* 4.20.7 (in *The Ante-Nicene Fathers*, eds. Alexander Roberts et al. [Buffalo, NY: Christian Literature, 1885], 1:489).

example.[7] If this is true of inanimate creatures, how much greater is the potential of covenanted, living, breathing beings created after the image of God to function in a sacramental way, together showing forth God's glory? If papyrus and electronic digits can mediate God's word to us, if wine and bread shows his presence, if oil pours forth his healing power, how much more can the human couple, especially one sanctified by the Holy Spirit and living in Christ, become an epiphany?

Indeed, it is not too speculative to suggest that this is what Adam and Eve were made to do. Created after the image of God, the divine intention was that they might together attain to his likeness and embody his glory in the created world. As my mentor Bishop Tom Wright likes to put it, "the Incarnation is not a category error."[8] Rather, it is the central event of our story that shines a spotlight not only on the character of God, but the character of humanity and our relationship to God's creation.

It is not insignificant, for example, that God the Son was born as a male of a woman. He assumed everything that we are, including the human state of a gendered condition. Some contemporary scholars have blended together feminist concerns with the patristic dictum "what is not assumed is not healed," and worried that, in not appearing as a woman, God could not have assumed femininity. To this quandary, several ingenious but unhelpful suggestions have been forthcoming: that Christ was, like Adam as conceived by some ancient rabbis, androgynous;[9] that we should reimagine him in our postmodern age in terms of a "Christa" as well; that the Christian story has a fatal, and central, misogynistic flaw, and should therefore be abandoned; that Jesus' sexuality was unrelated to his being.

---

7. Alexander Schmemann, *For the Life of the World: Sacraments and Orthodoxy* (1997; Yonkers, NY: St. Vladimir's, 2018), 142.

8. I have not found this exact phrase in his writings, but remember it from lively graduate classes with N. T. Wright.

9. For a summary of the rabbinic haggadic and halakhic material, see Moses Gaster's entry "Androgynous," in the 1906 Jewish Encyclopedia, available online at http://www.jewishencyclopedia.com/articles/1508-androgynos-hermaphrodite. For an example of a contemporary thinker who has followed this lead, see Paul Evdokimov, *Woman and the Salvation of the World: A Christian Anthropology on the Charisms of Women* (1983; New York; St. Vladimir's, 1994). Evdokimov postulates that the male person and the female person are two halves that must find completion in each other, and accordingly speculates about the resurrected state, finding help not only in the rabbis and some fathers, but also (more dubiously) in Swedenborg: "Swedenborg gives a luminous explanation of [Jesus' words in Mark 12:25]: the masculine and the feminine (in their totality) find one another again in the form of one single angel" (184).

All of these responses fall short in two respects. First, they ignore the key part that the Theotokos played in the incarnation. Even the earliest texts speak of Christ being "born of a woman" (Gal 4:4) and give (even embarrassing) detail concerning her status as the only human parent of God the Son. Biologically, this leads the contemporary thinker to an even deeper wonder than his or her first-century counterpart. They knew that conception without the coming together of a male and female was exceptional; our understanding of genetics makes it even more surprising. How does a human with XY chromosomes come from XX alone? In cases where we have seen natural parthenogenesis to be possible, it is a female bearing a female. Further, our faith does not suggest that Mary was a simple host, or incubator, but that her bearing of Christ was a full conception, and that she is the one from whom Christ took human flesh. It is surely significant, then, that the female sex was so intimately involved in the incarnation, and that the assumption of all things human by God the Son means his taking flesh *from her*. This puts a particular accent on Saint Paul's words that "for as woman came from man, so also man is born of woman" (1 Cor 11:12), and the words of the pastorals that there salvation comes through *teknogonia*, "through the bearing of a child" (1 Tim 2:15). Though both epistles are clearly speaking about the role of women in general, it is quite likely that behind this celebrated charism of woman stands the holy woman who was to become known as the "second Eve"—that one who said "yes" as an antidote to the primal "no."

It seems, then, that in tracing this mystery of our gendered condition, and in adequately expounding it, there are several missteps to be avoided. The first is that we cannot think of our state as male or female as an added or secondary feature to our humanity. This is belied both by our protology and our eschatology. It is a mistake to think of Adam as primarily androgynous, and as male/female as a secondary thing, or a declension from the beginning. After all, God said that it was *not* good for Adam to be alone, and the first statement of creation mentions male and female in a single breath. As for the final state of human beings, we might be tempted, on the basis of Jesus' words to the Sadducees, to sideline our gendered state.

It is true that some read his rejoinder (Mark 12:24–27; Luke 20:34–39) as instruction upon theological anthropology, including a dismissal of marriage in the final kingdom. What if, instead, we read it as Jesus' characteristically poignant response to the way that the Sadducees sarcastically framed their question? They have asked, after an exaggerated tale about seven brothers, "*Whose* wife will she be?" Jesus responds obliquely, as he does with the question of Caesar and the coin, "You don't know the power of God or the resurrection." It isn't like that.... She doesn't *belong* to anyone, since there is no giving or taking there, but "they are like the angels. Furthermore [in Luke's version] they won't die." So he declared that the effects of the fall—undue power of a man over his wife, and death—don't pertain in the resurrection. It is not at all clear that Jesus meant his words to form a qualifying statement regarding the continued relationship between husband and wife, joined together by God. Rather, he was challenging the ridicule and disbelief of the Sadducees, with their caricature of the resurrection as mere resuscitation, complete with sexual intercourse and reproduction. We cannot assume, on the basis of Jesus' answer, that male and female have no meaning at the consummation of all things. That is to push the text to carry a weight beyond what it can naturally bear.

As we think about human sexuality, it would seem that there is a middle ground between what we would call "essential" and what we would call "characteristic." Here the Western distinction between "essential" versus "accidental" does not serve us well. The maleness or femaleness of a particular human being is *neither* essential to his or her humanity, *nor* merely an outward accident (or appearance) of that one's identity, like my original wavy hair now turned, through the vicissitudes of medical treatment, almost kinky! No, our gendered condition fits neither into the category of essential nor accidental. For example, Genesis does not lead us to see the woman Eve as a *second* creation, separate from humanity—but she is distinct from Adam. Saint John the Golden-Mouthed explains that she is distinct in her *relationship*, especially since the fall, but not in her *nature*.[10] Further, Jesus, our second Adam, recapitulates all that it is to be human, *both* Adam and Eve, despite his male gender, and their particularities. Jesus is fully male, for he is a particular human being; but, as we have seen, his humanity is drawn exclusively from the woman. Moreover, as the second Adam, he retraces the steps of all of humanity. We are led to be amazed at a mystery!

Looking forward to the fulfillment of all things, I think it too bold to assume that at that time gendered distinctions will be obscured or will disappear. Those who worship in the church consider the risen and

---

10. My emphasis. "Homily 26" in *Homilies on the Epistle of Paul to the Corinthians* in *A Select Library of Nicene and Post-Nicene Fathers of the Christian Church*, ed. Philip Schaff (New York: Christian Literature Company, 1989), 12:150.

ascended Christ to be masculine, the Theotokos feminine, and the saints intact in their gendered natures. The fathers *have* differed regarding the glorified body, whether it retains sexual characteristics or not.[11] But in our worship, our reverence for our elder brothers and sisters, and our icons, we are encouraged by the church to relate to those who are glorified as masculine and feminine. It may be helpful to posit a distinction here between *physical* maleness and femaleness (complete with sexual organs) and the masculine and feminine as something larger, not confined to grammatical or social convention, and also not just abstract. Though it may not be entirely clear from the Scriptures and Holy Tradition whether the physical male and female characteristics themselves are eternal, it would seem that the distinction between masculine and feminine is something that persists. Woven into the theological grammar of the Scriptures, and our worship, is the idea that gendered language points to a mystery even bigger than that of a male and female in a single marriage: though that is *very* good!

And so we turn to the thorny problem of how our language can best speak of God, and of humanity. As I worked through this question in reading and rereading the books of C. S. Lewis, I posited several "boundaries" (to which I have added one for the purposes of this study), which I think may safeguard our thinking and our speculation on this mystery.[12] This action was prompted by the conviction that human beings, singly, married, and all together, are indeed mysterious. For the contemplation of mystery, Christians have a time honored tradition, evident, for example, in our creeds. Ancients concerned to respect that which is mysterious have typically marked off where we *cannot* and *must not* go, while we explore what we can of the remarkable truth under consideration. Our holy God is, for example, *un*created, *im*mortal, *un*containable, *without* parts and passions, and so on. In harmony with this principle, I offer nine suggestions to guide our conversations about theological anthropology. A few of these nine boundaries may be controversial in an egalitarian age

---

11. For differences among the fathers regarding the retention of personal characteristics in the eschaton, including the elements of gender and sexual organs, see Elizabeth Clark, *The Origenist Controversy: The Cultural Construction of an Early Christian Debate* (Princeton: Princeton University Press, 1992), and Carolyn Walker Bynum, *The Resurrection of the Body in Western Christianity 200–1336* (New York: Columbia University Press, 1995).

12. Edith M. Humphrey, *Further Up and Further In: Orthodox Conversations with C. S. Lewis on Scripture and Theology* (Yonkers, NY: St. Vladimir's Press, 2017), 271–272.

that wants to adopt a wholly non-hierarchical Godhead as its mascot, but I believe that all of these are borne out by Scriptures, Holy Tradition, and even our own experience:

II. God, Human Beings, and Language: Some Boundaries

The first two boundaries may be taken as a pair:

- We cannot say that all symbols are merely human expressions, and that language and action are detachable from the reality to which they point.
- We cannot say that gendered language is expendable in talking about God or humanity.

These first two hedges mark out the potential of created things to indicate, and to share sacramentally, in the reality who is God. Certainly there are some symbols that are merely arbitrary and functional: the sign for a women's restroom, for example, or a red octagonal that signals "STOP." Linguists know that not all words that we use are onomatopoeic, sharing in what they denote by their sound. Similarly, Christians do not hold to pantheism, which assumes that the creation, by its nature, shares in, and indeed composes, something that is divine. But, as Romans 1:18–21 tells us, God has so created the universe that it is designed specifically to point to something, indeed to Someone, beyond itself, even while retaining its own life or significance. This must surely be part of what the apostle means in speaking about husband and wife as *really* expressing the mystery of Christ and his church (Eph 5:32). And since the gendered language in pointing to this wonder is so pervasive in the Scriptures, beginning with the hint that Adam and Eve are created after God's image and ending with the marriage of the Lamb, it is very unlikely that this particular metaphor is something expendable.

To call Christ "she" and the church "he," following the line of, say, the children's book *The Paper Bag Princess*, would be to distort the story.[13] And to drop all gendered language, in favor of "it" or multiple

---

13. Robert Munsch, *The Paper Bag Princess* (Clive, IA: Turtleback, 1999), has delighted many in our day with its reversal plot, in which Elizabeth, the princess, saves her betrothed Ronald, who has been abducted. Its amusement relies upon the recognition of a reversal, of course, and would not be humorous to those who do not know the traditional ordering of such stories.

neutral titles, would be to kill the story. Since we cannot get outside of the Church to compare her to things feminine, or outside of God to compare his divinity with things masculine, we take a great risk in linguistically spading and gelding the partners. What might we be losing besides our continuity with past generations? We cannot say with precision, but it might be a considerable loss!

The next two boundaries also can be paired.

- We cannot say that the relations of Father, Son and Spirit are symmetrical, nor can we say that they are not mutual and equal.
- We cannot say that the relations of husband and wife are totally symmetrical, nor ought we to say that there is no mutuality or equality.

These have to do with the strange relations that we find both in the Godhead and also in the married couple, to which Saint Paul alludes in 1 Corinthians 11. In the past twenty years there has been a heated controversy in evangelical circles on "hierarchy in the Trinity," with the most recent salvo being launched by the collection of essays entitled *Trinity without Hierarchy*, edited by Michael Bird and Scott Harrower. This debate appears to have been catalyzed originally by the analogy drawn by complementarians such as Wayne Grudem and Bruce Ware[14] between the Persons of the Holy Trinity and the role of males and females in the church. Their use of 1 Corinthians 11 enraged egalitarians, who then charged them with the heresy of subordinationism: from the egalitarian perspective, their fellow more traditionalist evangelicals had no proper patristic or biblical ground to stand upon. The obvious difficulty with this charge is that 1 Corinthians 11 explicitly declares an eternal (and not just economic) hierarchy in speaking of Father and Son—even the Son has a head, the Father, argues the apostle, and so women should not be ashamed to acknowledge headship in their husbands. *Hierarchy* in itself need not be eschewed as a dirty word, but simply means "holy origin" or "holy head."

Of course, there is a heretical form of subordinationism, as was made clear in the Arian debates, and so *Trinity without Hierarchy* has also enlisted the support of some non-egalitarians who are worried about this error. However, both 1 Corinthians 11:1–16 and 1 Corinthians 15:24–28

---

14. For example, see Wayne Grudem, ed., *Biblical Foundations for Manhood and Womanhood* (Wheaton, IL: Crossway, 2002) and Bruce Ware, "Male and Female Complementarity and the Image of God," in Grudem, *Biblical Foundations*, 71–92.

speak about the willing submission of the Son to the Father in eternity: in the eschaton, and not simply during his earthly life, "He will give all things over to the Father." Similarly, it is the delight of the Holy Spirit to honor the Father and the Son, and not to attract attention to himself. Indeed, though radical subordinationism has been declared a heresy since the time of Arius, not a few ancient fathers speak about the *monarchia*[15] as residing most properly with the Father, since he is the *eternal source* of the Son and the Holy Spirit.

The relationship between Father, Son, and Holy Spirit, then, is ordered, and yet each and together the Persons are God, mutual, equally deserving of honor and worship, and each honoring the Other. In an ineffable mystery, holy order and mutuality come together. The relations

---

15. Some have, in this debate, appealed to St. Gregory of Nazianzus to refute hierarchy in the Godhead. For example, Kevin Giles et al. (*The Trinity & Subordinationism: The Doctrine of God & the Contemporary Gender Debate* [Downers Grove, IL: InterVarsity, 2002] and *Jesus and the Father*) seems catalyzed by concerns of social egalitarianism and reads Gregory according to this focus. Robert Letham (*The Holy Trinity: In Scripture, History, Theology and Worship* [Phillipsburg, NJ: P&R Publishing, 2004]) is more measured, and accepts the term *taxis*, but not hierarchy. T. F. Torrance's work (*The Trinitarian Faith: The Evangelical Theology of the Ancient Catholic Church* [Edinburgh: T. & T. Clark, 1995] and "The Doctrine of the Holy Trinity—Gregory Nazianzen and John Calvin," *Calvin Studies* 5, edited by John H. Leith and W. Stacy Johnson, 7–19 [Richmond, VA: Union Theological Seminary, 1995]) is, in my view, mostly sane, and wonderfully vigorous. Especially I am grateful to Torrance for his careful refutation of the idea of *perichōresis* as a "circular dance." However, his objection to an orthodox form of subordination in the Trinity does not seem to cohere with this understanding of *perichōresis*. He champions Saint Gregory of Nazianzus over against the other Cappadocians in the matter of *taxis*, but neglects where the saint speaks of the monarchy of the Father and of the sense in which he is "greater" than the Son. Most recently, Peter J. Leithart, in "No Son, No Father" (*Trinity without Hierarchy*, 119–21) has argued that *taxis* and hierarchy should be differentiated, pleading that *taxis* does not imply authority, whereas hierarchy does. Appealing to Athanasius (who obviously was countering the Arian controversy) Leithart problematically imports necessity into the divine communion, confusing the logical and necessary causes (i.e., the Father *needs* the Son to be Father!). We might further comment that to take *kephalē* and *archē* as simple descriptions of origin *may* work when we are speaking of the in-time relationship of husband and wife; but what can *primacy* possibly mean between Father and Son except a primacy of honor, when there is no temporal element involved? (Of course, this primacy is paradoxically complemented in the Scriptures and the fathers by the recognition of mutuality and equal divinity among the Persons of the Trinity). It is helpful to remember that the concept of Father as both *aitia* (cause) and *archē* (font; beginning) is common to both the Roman Catholic and the Orthodox communion. The burden of proof therefore lies with those Protestants who, in dissent from this view, urge a radical qualification or even denial of *taxis* in the Godhead, such as the title "Trinity without Hierarchy" implies.

are not symmetrical: Father is not begotten, Son does not beget, Holy Spirit does not cause procession, yet they enjoy utter mutuality and are One. It should be mentioned as well that the scholarly urban myth that *perichōresis* means a "round dance" is badly mistaken. The *perichōresis* of the Holy Trinity is a patristic doctrinal term that portrayed the unique way in which Father, Son, and Holy Spirit make room for and indwell each other. *Perichoresis,* spelled with an omicron (a short o) does evoke the idea of the dancing of the Chorus in Greek tragedy and is applied a few times in the ancient literature to the praises of the cherubim in heaven. But the *perichōresis* of the Trinity is a different word, spelled with an omega (a long o). All too frequently, theologians have carelessly appealed to this misspelled and mistaken term, as though the Trinitarian *perichōresis* could mitigate or remove the embarrassment of the *taxis* (dare I say hierarchy?) that is apparent between Father, Son, and Holy Spirit. This would be to flatten out the mystery, to make it more palatable for our day. No, the tension stands: hierarchy alongside mutuality.

This kind of tension also appears in the way the Scriptures depict man-and-woman. They are created together, and both given the task of ruling, yet Adam is the human source and head: he names Eve. In Ephesians, both mutual submission (5:21), and the special submission of wife (5:22–24) *with* the special sacrifice of husband (5:25–26), are indicated. Order and mutuality come together in a way that we find difficult to fathom. Past ages no doubt overemphasized the order, and valorized the domination precipitated by the fall (Gen 3:16), rather than the "no male and female" celebrated by Galatians 3:28. Our day, of course, does the opposite, allowing the "no male and female" phrase to silence the household rules, and to avoid the spiritual grammar implied in the mirroring of Christ and the church by male and female spouses.

Let us move on to three more boundaries that may be grouped together conceptually.

- We cannot say that woman and man are two different creations, but we also cannot say man and woman are indistinct from each other.
- We cannot say that there is an absolutely confined role for each gender; reversals are part of our story.
- We cannot say that there are no "higher" gifts and no "lesser" gifts, but all are necessary, and the higher need the lower, so that sometimes it is impossible to discern which is more important.

The first may seem self-evident, but it has not always been seen as such, nor is it today accepted in all quarters.[16] Some have so stressed the second part of the creation narrative, the detailed one, that they have forgotten the clear words of Genesis 1, and Jesus' summary of this in the Gospels: "in the beginning He created them, male and female." Eve is clearly described as sharing her origin with Adam, and the image of God with Adam: she is not created separately out of the earth by the LORD but brought out of Adam. They are created together, even though one precedes the other. The responsibilities and charisms that God bequeaths Adam are also those of Eve, for they are one flesh.

Saint John Chrysostom, in expounding Ephesians 5, warns men against taking the household rules in such a way that they distance themselves from their wives in an ontological sense: "For what if the wife be under subjection to us? It is as a wife, as free, as equal in honor. And the Son also, though He did become obedient to the Father, it was as the Son of God, it was as God."[17] (Later in the homily, he points out that radical submission was accentuated because of the woman's disobedience, and was not foundational; moreover, as he concludes, he chastises those who express male domination in terms of violence or physical discipline of wives.) The Golden-mouthed reminds us: just as Father and Son are equally and together God, yet distinct, so man and woman share a mutual nature that should inform their relationship. (Of course, both the unity and personhood of male and female are merely faint echoes of the ineffable unity and distinctness of the Trinitarian Persons.)

What about roles, as touched upon in the second of this triad? Certainly, male and female persons have, throughout human experience, and in the Scriptures, taken on (in some cases, with God's own appointing)

---

16. I should confess that I have not had time to examine the work of the complementarians themselves on this point but have only responded to how they are depicted and characterized by the egalitarians. It may be that some of them do not heed this boundary, and so have slipped into too rigid a view of male and female functions or roles, without room for reversals as given exceptionally by God. Those who read scholars on the conservative side of this debate may want to examine their statements against these boundaries: if the Son is only like and not of the same nature as the Father, then woman may be understood as like, but not of the same nature as the man. However, the charge of "quasi-homoianism" made by some in *Trinity without Hierarchy* does not seem to be substantiated by the arguments in that volume. (See, for example, Bird's introduction, which asserts this heresy but does not demonstrate it.)

17. "Homily 26" in *Homilies on the Epistle of Paul to the Corinthians* in *A Select Library of Nicene and Post-Nicene Fathers of the Christian Church*, ed. Philip Schaff (New York: Christian Literature Company, 1989), 12:150.

specific roles. It is not for a father to bear and nurse a child; it is not normative for a mother (I would argue, anyway) to protect the family by bearing arms, though extremity may lead to unusual situations. The "enstatic" tendency of woman, to operate within a certain sphere and bear mysteries within, and the "ecstatic" tendency of man, to go beyond the boundaries of the family in sacrificial effort, are not absolute, however![18] The people of God have had the experience of honoring contemplative saints who are male, and warrior saints who are female. Indeed, the book of Proverbs describes the ideal woman in terms of one who is enterprising, and who goes *outside* of her family in order to build it up!

In salvation history, moreover, we see specific approved examples of what we could consider to be a "reversal" of the usual state of affairs. This is not only true in the ordering of male and female: consider how the gentiles, who were supposed to be given light by Israel (Isa 60:3), take on the primary role in making the Jewish people jealous, as narrated in Romans 10:19 and 11:11-14. With male and female it is also the case. Deborah becomes a judge. Women (and unusual women, at that!) find their way into Matthew's genealogy of Jesus. Rahab is included in Hebrews' list of heroes (Heb 11:31), where we would expect, according to the sequence, Joshua: she provides a poignant and astonishing type for Jesus, since as a gentile she dwelt "outside the camp" of the Israelites (Josh 6:23), while Jesus suffered "outside the camp" for the entire world (Heb 13:13). We envision an unexpected possibility when Saint Paul asks of the Christian wife, "How do you know, O wife, whether you will save your (unbelieving) husband?" (1 Cor 7:16). Finally, Saint Paul remarks both on the natural reversal of the original created order, and the radicalizing presence of God as the author of all, in 1 Corinthians 11:

> For man was not made from woman, but woman from man.
> Neither was man created for woman, but woman for man. . . .
> Nevertheless, in the Lord woman is not independent of man
> nor man of woman;
> for as woman was made from man, so man is now born of woman.
> And all things are from God. (1 Cor 11:8-12)

Here Saint Paul insists upon holding together truths in tension: the male first, yet now the female first in at least some respects, and in any

---

18. It would seem Paul Evdokimov, in *Woman and the Salvation*, overplays these male and female tendencies, yet nonetheless makes an interesting case that the man may be aligned typologically with the second Person of the Trinity, while the woman, in nature, matches the third Person of the Trinity, as evident in her charisms.

case, God is first. We cannot co-opt Saint Paul (or indeed, the Scriptures as a whole) either for domination politics in the Christian household, or for egalitarianism. He (and they) will not be pinned down.

The insights put forward by the first two of this triad would appear to be predicated on the third. We have a sense that there is an ordering of gifts (cf. 1 Cor 14:1), and so also an "ordering" of those who hold these gifts, and yet every gift is important (1 Cor 12:15). Things are not always as they seem. We learn this even in the Old Testament, where David the lowly is selected in his tribe, and where we hear that "God does not look on the outward appearance" (1 Sam 16:7). It is amplified in the New Testament by a focus upon Jesus as the Suffering Servant and dying Messiah, and then extended in Saint Paul's description of his followers: "God chose what is foolish in the world to shame the wise, God chose what is weak in the world to shame the strong, God chose what is low and despised in the world, even things that are not, to bring to nothing things that are, so that no human being might boast in the presence of God" (1 Cor 1:27–29). Reversals, then, are part of salvation history, and also the very makeup in the church; thus they find an honored place in male-female relations.

Let us move all to the last two boundaries, in which we consider specifically how we should speak about God, and the tradition of using gendered language to do so.

- In God-talk, we cannot forbid the use of feminine imagery, for the Bible uses it.

- In God-talk, we cannot ignore the usual or normative use of masculine language, even if it is uncomfortable to us.

Please notice that the first "hedge" speaks specifically about feminine *imagery*. That is, the Bible, both Old Testament and New Testament, uses the language of simile, in comparing God to the female. God is *like* a nursing mother, *like* a midwife, *like* a mother hen yearning to protect her children in Jerusalem, *like* a woman searching for a coin.[19] Nowhere is the pronoun "she" used explicitly for God, and nowhere is an unadorned female metaphor or title used. Yet the feminine pictures are there. If we feel no compunction in using the parable of the prodigal son to point out the "prodigal" generosity of our heavenly Father, we should feel no

---

19. Some have commented that Luke 15:8–10 does not intend to make an analogy between God and the woman who rejoices. Though the joy is specifically related to the hosts of heaven, the parable follows on the heels of the rejoicing Shepherd and begins with "just so." It seems perverse to forbid this connection.

compunction about using this other language as well. It is part of the repertoire of human language that God sanctifies for us as we try to understand and communicate all that he is. Eve mirrors him, the true Giver of Life, the only Wise Counsellor, the tender Nurturer of his children. Those of us who are conservative in temperament are not at liberty to ignore this accent in the Scriptures, even given the topsy-turvy values of our day.

Yet the final boundary must stay firmly in place. Masculine language is normative, not simply for the Son, but for the Father, and for the Holy Spirit—the gender of whom, if dictated by Hebrew, should be female, or if dictated by Greek, should be neuter. Jesus, in his teaching on the Holy Spirit, surprisingly uses the Greek masculine pronoun *ekeinos* in referring to him and his work, and not the more grammatically natural neuter pronoun (John 14:26; 15:26). We cannot take the route of "cultural accommodation" and assume that Jesus was hampered by his time and would have used Mother or other more congenial metaphors if he had come in our time. "Father" (*Abba*) is the most characteristic name of our God, raised by Jesus from a mere metaphor among others to the mystery which we may be bold to declare, if we are in him. He is "his Father" and therefore "Our Father."[20] To relegate this to a cultural matter is to lose one of the most mysterious aspects of our faith. If we find it uncomfortable, because of difficulty with a human father, or the scorn of our age, it may be helpful to remember that Ephesians 3:15 puts the heavenly Father forth as the source and pattern of *every* sort of "fatherhood" (*patria*) in heaven and on earth.[21] Meddle with this metaphor, and we may be touching mysteries we can scarcely grasp!

These nine negative statements are designed to give us some parameters, guarding from danger and retaining the mysteries involved in our gendered condition, as well as in the gendered language that we rightly use of God. There is an urgency, it would seem, to probe *and* to guard the mystery of male and female in order to give answers to our sexually confused age: we want to remain in Christ, to learn more and more of him and our world, and to commend what is real and true to others. It is

20. I would be remiss not to credit Garrett Green as my original mentor, back in the 1990s, for his astute and poetic depiction of the intractable and astounding masculine language used by Scripture for God. See his "The Gender of God and the Theology of Metaphor" in *Speaking the Christian God: The Holy Trinity and the Challenge of Feminism*, ed. A. Kimel (Grand Rapids: Eerdmans, 1992), 44-64.

21. Even those who translate *patria* as "household," rather than the abstract noun "fatherhood," must admit that the term is constituted by reference to the *pater*, the father.

my prayer that these boundaries may be of service in our investigation and contemplation, as we seek to explain to our skeptical and egalitarian-driven age why the reality of male and female matters, and what Christian masculine and feminine language signifies (and does not signify) regarding our Creator.

No discussion of male and female, however, is complete without acknowledging the natural presence of children among two who, in the course of nature, become father and mother by virtue of their union.

III. The Significance of Children

Some have misguidedly thought it theologically significant that children only arrive after the fall, as if it is a fruit of the fall itself. Such detractors forget that the command to be fruitful and multiply came at the beginning, and not as a concession. Implicitly, just as it is not good for male and female to be alone, so it would not be good (or at least not *fully* good, not in the order of things) for male and female to be without children. Consider how the Old Testament acknowledges the pain of childless couples (and how God reverses this) and has a psalm that rejoices in "a quiver-full of children." Moreover, consider how our New Testament story begins with the plight of a barren woman, a cousin of Holy Mary, who miraculously and joyfully conceives. This surely is a metaphor, too, for barren Israel, who finally brings forth fruit.

As with sexuality, we might be tempted to think that propagation is merely something that we share with the animals. This assumption forgets two key matters: first, every child conceived is not merely an animal, but one created after the likeness of God; second, God by his natural generosity, himself moves ecstatically out as Creator. It is possible here to play our cards too confidently in drawing a parallel between the divine and human actions. We want neither to downplay the work of God in the conception of a person, nor to picture an overly anthropomorphized God, who "can't help" but create because of his nature. However, the centrality of Father-Son language in our creed suggests that the parent-child link, no less than that of man and woman, has an iconic function. The human child is iconic of the relation between Father and Son; further, the child may be seen as picturing God's intimacy with us, and his overflowing abundance showered on us. Moreover, the way that a child enters the world shows forth our very human participation in God's creating activity. After all, we do not simply produce a *body*, but a whole child made in the image of God.

And, if we are Christian parents, we participate in that child's *re-creation*, as we bring her or him to baptism and the holy mysteries, nurture that one in Christ, and so on.

What could be more astonishing than Saint Paul's words to Christian mothers, "but as it is, [your children] are holy" (1 Cor 7:14)? I am not here picking a bone with Saint Augustine, who in his treatise "On Original Sin" reminds the Christian couple that they do not bring forth recreated offspring, but those in solidarity with Adam.[22] It is true that Christian parents do not automatically conceive children of the new creation! (I probably would, however, in another context, like to say something about Saint Augustine's construal of original guilt and his influence on the Western view of this matter.) Here it suffices to remember Saint Peter's words on Pentecost to the listening crowd: "This promise is to you and your children" (Acts 2:39). In the normal flow of events, Christian parents not only bear children created after the image of God but can hope and act so that their beloved ones grow and mature, attaining to the likeness of God in Christ. Male and female, in the created order, were meant to bring forth new life. Believing husband and wife are meant to raise children in the joy of recreated newness of life. Moreover, children have their own lessons to teach their fallen parents: lessons about innocence, about receiving the kingdom of God with simplicity, about trust and vulnerability, and more basically, about the intrinsic fruitfulness of love. Whenever we have offspring, we have before us a vivid picture of the rich and endless giving of our loving God. We learn in our own experience, "it is not good for Adam (and Eve) to be alone." Yet, in speaking of the gift of children to those who are married, we must hasten to add a caveat. For in the body of Christ there are notable exceptions.

IV. Exceptions That Prove the Rule: Childless Couples and Singles

Each of these estates, childlessness and singleness, has an honored place in the church. Chosen singleness is obvious as a Christian good, since Jesus (and Saint Paul) valorized celibacy, pointing out the way of the

---

22. Chapters 43–48 of Augustine, "On Original Sin," in *Basic Writings of Saint Augustine*, ed. Whitney J. Oates (New York: Random House, 1948), 1:650–54.

spiritual eunuch as a special grace, given to some. Both Saint Paul (who probably as a rabbi had a living wife at some point) and the LORD make it abundantly clear that a fully human and complete life is to be had for those who are single, and who honor God in their singleness (cf. Matt 9:12; 1 Cor 7:1). Especially in our sex-crazed age, the witness and ministry of godly celibate men and women is essential. Yes, married couples have an iconic function, pointing to Christ and the church, but there is more to the mystery of the kingdom than this one aspect. Further, some of what it is to be male and female will no doubt pass away. The celibate person gives a necessary accent, or corrective, to the normative life of humanity, reminding us that our current situation, though "good," points to something we can scarcely imagine. We do not yet know the full story, or the full glory, to which we are called. Those of us who are caught up in the cultural fight for the family must never forget that our place as married couples with children is, to some extent, exigent (though blessed). There is only one thing necessary: to worship at the feet of Christ. And, in some ways, the single person can do this with more devotion.

And what of the childlessness that some couples face? Though significant arguments must be made that childlessness should not be a chosen situation, we know all too well that God brings good things out of sorrow and weakness. This state, too, can bring glory to God, for that couple is now free to adopt young ones who have needs in this heartless age, or, so to speak, to conceive spiritual "children" in the church. Consider Jesus, the single male, who speaks in Hebrews about "me and the children the Lord has given me" (Heb 2:13), or Paul's characteristic use of "father" in naming his relationship with the churches. Remember, also, that breathtaking glory of that "ordinary" but glorified woman Sarah, in Lewis's *The Great Divorce*,[23] accompanied by a colorful train of young ones, whom she had made her children in her daily nurturing contact with them. Though effectively without a husband (the ghostly "Tragedian," who seemingly dissolves into nothingness, does not count!), she has the charisms of a mother!

Finally, then, we return to our first thought, that male and female, along with the children that come from this union, are a good in themselves, but point to something far greater. Their greatest role is to be iconic, pointing to the deep mystery of masculine and feminine, glimpsed in Christ and the church, but perhaps found also in other unseen (cosmic?

---

23. C. S. Lewis, *The Great Divorce* (1946; Glasgow: Collins Fontana, 1972, fifth impression 1975), 118–19.

angelic?) realities about which we have very little knowledge at this time. Male-and-female, God's very good creation, is not alone, but accompanied by the work and gift of children, both physical and spiritual, and embodied in a rich and teaming universe, the inhabitants of which we do not yet fully see! Yet in our spiritual naiveté, we are even now surrounded by this cloud of witnesses and these dumbfounding unseen powers, as we live in Christ. Ours is a humble and honored position, in which we may rejoice. We are not alone as we struggle to remain faithful in the midst of current challenges to what we have learned both about ourselves and the God who made us. There is beauty in the simplicity of our human lives, and there is depth in the spiritual mysteries to which we, in our various conditions and relations, point.

> For each perfect Gift of Thine
> To our race so freely given,
> Graces human and Divine,
> Flowers of earth, and buds of Heaven:
> Christ, our God, to Thee we raise
> This our Sacrifice of Praise.

(Folliott S. Pierpoint, "For the Beauty of the Earth," 1864)[24]

---

24. Those who love this hymn may be surprised to discover that only the stanzas that refer to the earthly joys are usually retained in the singing of our congregations. The full hymn contains eight stanzas, and opens up the mysterious connections between human love and the loves of heaven, by detailing the ecclesial Bride, the glorified martyrs, righteous prophets, and virgins, all of whom are seen as types of the ultimate sacrifice of Christ.

5

Body, Soul, Resurrection, and Heaven

Patrick Lee

WHAT IS CHRISTIAN TEACHING about what a human being is? This question can arise in different contexts, for example, when speaking about the beginning of life, the end of life, or sexual morality. But one important context raising this question is in thinking about the resurrection of all human beings. Another—though often it is only implicitly touched on—is in one's notion of heaven. Here I will focus on these two issues—the resurrection of all human beings and heaven—and indicate how our notion of what constitutes a human person is important for these core components of Christian life.

I.

Scripture has traditionally been interpreted as teaching, or implying, both that human beings are essentially bodily beings, and that their makeup includes a spiritual component, a soul. When God expels Adam from Paradise, he tells him, "For you are dust and unto dust you shall return" (Gen 3:19),[1] suggesting that matter is part of what we are.

---

1. In the prologue to Saint John's Gospel the evangelist declares that "the Word became flesh and dwelt amongst us," thus implying that having flesh is part of human nature. When Our Lord discusses the nature of marriage, he begins by reaffirming Genesis's teaching on marriage: "When a man leaves his father and mother and clings

Genesis teaches that when God created the human being, God formed him from the dust of the earth, and then blew into his nostrils the breath of life (Gen 2:7). This has traditionally been interpreted as indicating that God directly created the human being's spiritual soul, infusing it into his body.² Indeed, the Catholic Church has defined that a human being is composed of body and soul, that the soul is related to the body as form to matter, and that the human soul is naturally immortal.³

If a human being's makeup somehow involves both body and soul, the question arises as to how these are related to each other. And this problem arises in a pressing way when thinking about the resurrection of human persons. We die, which means the soul is separated from the body. Then at the end of the world, that is, after a certain time or interval, we are raised from the dead. What are we to say about the human being during that interim duration?

Of course, there are different interpretations of the doctrine of the resurrection, but I will assume here that it is meant as literally true. The body that one has after the resurrection is a glorified body, so there is an element of mystery in this belief. Nevertheless, I take it that the mystery does not remove the basic affirmation: at one time the body is in the grave and is dead, and at some later time the body—in *some* sense the same body—is alive, though of course there is discussion about what makes it the same body.

---

to his wife, the two become one flesh. And therefore what God has joined together let no man put asunder" (Matt 19:5–6). It seems that this becoming one flesh could scarcely have such profound impact or significance if the human person were not in herself a bodily being. Also see Saint Paul in 1 Corinthians 6:12–20.

2. This point—that the human being has a spiritual component—is also suggested by the teaching that human beings are made in the image and likeness of God, and that they are given dominion over all other material things (Gen 1:26–31). Thus human beings are different in kind, not just in degree from other material things. This point may suggest that human beings have a special, spiritual component.

It might also be argued that this point is implied by the teaching that human beings have free choice. Entrance into the kingdom of God, or communion with God, is a free gift offered to us, and it is taught that we are free to accept it, with God's grace, or reject it. But the actions of purely material things—speaking of actions at the macro-level here and setting aside the quantum level of material things—seem to be determined by the antecedent material forces acting on them. And so our choice to accept or our choice to reject—in other words, our free choice—seems to be something other than a material event.

3. See *Catechism of the Catholic Church*, #365.

At this point an obvious question or objection arises: if you and I are bodily beings—that is, if the body is essential to what a human being is—then it seems that the human being ceases to be at death, that is, goes completely out of existence. But is that possible?

There are various ways of answering this question. I'll consider four: Platonism, physicalism, Thomas Aquinas's position, and a modification of Aquinas's position. The last position is the one I recommend. I will not be able to provide decisive reasons for my recommendation, but I will offer some partial justifications, and along the way we will see some pros and cons for each of the four positions.

One view of what a human being is, is the Platonist or Cartesian position. On this view, what I am is a soul, and I possess a body, as an extrinsic instrument. The body is not part of me, but it is an extrinsic entity with which I interact.[4] This view may seem to be a simpler answer to the problem posed by the interim between death and resurrection. For on this view there is no problem of a gap in existence. I do not cease to exist at one time and then come to be, as the same individual, at a later time. Rather, I am a soul, and death, though traumatic, is merely the loss of an external possession.

However, there are difficulties for a Christian Platonist position. First, as I mentioned above, Scripture seems to say that dust is part of our makeup. Yet how can it be true on the Platonist position that I *am* dust and that I will return to it? It seems, rather, that Platonism is the precise denial of that assertion.[5]

Moreover, if what I am is a purely spiritual entity, then my connection to a body is inessential or extrinsic. It is difficult to see on the Platonist or Cartesian view how union with the body could be something good for the soul. On the Platonist view it seems that union with the body must be either a punishment of the soul or perhaps for the body's benefit,

---

4. Descartes at times articulates a view that holds that body is part of the human being rather than a possession, but I am taking his view as it is standardly interpreted, that is, according to which the human being is the mind or soul, and the body is an extrinsic entity with which the mind, the self, interacts.

5. Also, Catholics have the teaching of the Church excluding the Platonist or Cartesian position. The Council of Vienne taught that the rational soul is *per se* the form of the body, and *The Catechism of the Catholic Church* teaches, "The unity of soul and body is so profound that one has to consider the soul to be the 'form' of the body: i.e., it is because of its spiritual soul that the body made of matter becomes a living, human body; spirit and matter, in man, are not two natures united, but rather their union forms a single nature." *Catechism of the Catholic Church*, #365.

but not something that benefits the soul, or something that the soul needs according to its own nature or constitution. But, in that case, it is hard to see why the resurrection should be so important to begin with. And it is clear that the resurrection has always been central to Christian belief.

A second position on how the body and soul are related is materialism or physicalism. This is the view that there is no spiritual component referred to as the soul. Perhaps what is referred to when people speak of the soul or mind is the intelligent behaviors performed by the human organism, or the particular organ of the human being—her brain—that enables her to perform intelligent behaviors. On this view, human beings are highly organized material organisms and there is no need to posit an additional spiritual component.

According to this position one must say that at death the human person ceases to be. But how can a person cease to be, and then that numerically same human person come back into existence at a later time? There seems to be something at least problematical about that.

This is particularly a difficulty for the physicalist view. On the physicalist Christian view there seems to be no ontological continuity at all between the me that dies and the me that is resurrected. Suppose you take your watch apart, and you leave the parts on the table for awhile, and then later reassemble them. Is that the same watch? It seems reasonable to say that it is. The continuity between the disassembled watch and the reassembled watch at least makes it somewhat plausible to think so.

But suppose you disassemble the watch, lose all of its parts, and then at a later time build a watch on the same design, shape, and size as the first watch. Is that the same watch? It doesn't seem so; it would seem to be a replica of the original watch rather than a reassembled or resurrected watch. And of course if our faith is not in vain then it must be me that is raised from the dead, not someone who just looks like me, or even someone who has memories that are qualitatively similar to the memories I now have. And it seems that without any continuity between what died and what is alive after the resurrection, it would be a replica of me and not me. Now this may not be correct; perhaps there could be identity without any continuity. What's intrinsically possible here isn't crystal clear. So, this is a difficulty, not an absolute refutation—still, it is a serious difficulty for the physicalist view.[6]

---

6. Various philosophers have defended a Christian materialist view on the resurrection. For example: Peter Van Inwagen, *The Possibility of Resurrection and Other Essays in Apologetics* (Boulder, CO: Westview, 1998), 45–51; Trenton Merricks, "How

A third view of what to say about the human being during the interim is that of Saint Thomas Aquinas. I believe his position is not only worthwhile but that most of it is correct. I will suggest, though, that an important modification to it is needed.[7] In any case, it will be worthwhile to look at his option in order to understand the issue, and along the way we will see some of the pros and cons of the other approaches to this issue.

What is distinctive of Saint Thomas's approach is that, on the one hand, he argues that I am not a soul but am a body-soul composite, and so he rejects the Platonist or Cartesian position. On the other hand, he argues that the soul is spiritual, that is, is independent for its existence in relation to the body, and that the soul survives death. In this way, he rejects a purely materialist or physicalist position. Let us view this position step by step.

Step one: following Aristotle on this point, Aquinas holds that the soul is related to the body as substantial form is related to matter. In material things we can distinguish between the matter or stuff that goes into the makeup of a thing, and another principle which specifies that matter to be of this kind rather than of another kind, called the substantial form. Aristotle famously compared these two components to the *bronze* out of

---

to Live Forever without Saving Your Soul," in *Soul, Body, and Survival: Essays on the Metaphysics of Human Persons*, ed. Kevin Corcoran (New York: Cornell University Press, 2001), 183–200.

However, if I could cease to be at time t1 and then God could recreate me at, say, time t10, without any continuity at all between me at t1 and me at t10 (no persisting components at all), then wouldn't that mean that it is possible (not logically contradictory) that God might also create a me at t2, another me at t3, still another at t4, without my previous me's ceasing to exist? But the second, third, or fourth me couldn't be me if I'm a previous one, by the law of identity. So it seems that *God's creating many me's* would be internally contradictory and thus logically impossible. This is not a limitation on God's power. Rather, God's omnipotence extends only to what is not an intrinsic contradiction, or to *what God's creating* would not be intrinsically contradictory. (*God's sinning*, to take another example, is internally contradictory, even though *sinning* is not internally contradictory.) So it looks like the possibility of God's recreating a numerically same individual, *where there is no continuity at all, no persistence of any components*, logically entails a contradiction, and so cannot be true. It is itself internally contradictory or logically impossible.

7. Others have suggested this point also. For example, David Hervshenov and Rose Koch-Hershenov, "Personal Identity and Purgatory," *Religious Studies* 42 (2006) 439–51; Christopher Tollefsen, "Brain Death and Irreplaceable Parts," *Life and Learning XXVI: Proceedings of the 2017 Conference of the University Faculty for Life* (2017), 23–35.

which a statue is made, and the *shape* that informs it. A statue is composed of bronze, which is of itself indeterminate, but is specified to be a statue by its shape. Analogously, the *matter* of a horse is indeterminate, and could go into the makeup of various things, but is specified to be a horse rather than something else by a principle called its *substantial form*. Thus a material thing is a composite: it is composed of matter on the one hand, and substantial form, on the other. The form is not the shape of a thing, but the principle—you could also call it the nature—which makes this matter to be this kind of thing rather than another, and also specifies the way this thing will typically act and react.

If the thing is a living being—whether it be plant, animal, or human—its form is called a *soul*. The soul is also the principle or component that organizes the various cells, tissues, and organs, making the organism one thing, one substance. The ultimate principle of unity cannot be a body since this would only give rise to an aggregate of this entity with other bodies (and so what make those components one thing would remain unexplained), but it must be a *form* determining the components to be one substantial entity. Thus, according to this approach each living being has a soul, and the soul is the substantial form or principle of unity in the thing.

So to say that in a human being the soul is related to the body as form is related to matter is to say that the soul is responsible for the thing's being alive, and that the soul is not the whole thing, but one component of the thing. The soul is just one component of the human being: the human being essentially includes matter as well as soul or form. The human soul is also the formal source of the living operations of a living being, such operations as growth, nourishment, perception, and—unique to human beings among material beings, as far as we know—understanding and willing.[8]

Second, Aquinas also holds that the soul is spiritual, that is, it is independent of matter for its existence, and so survives death. One argument he advances for this point is as follows. The human being performs certain actions that are independent of matter. That is, unlike actions such as walking or punching—which can only be performed with bodily organs—these are actions that are done without a bodily organ. For example, one cannot walk without legs with which one walks; one cannot

---

8. The subject that performs these actions is the living organism as a whole, and the soul is only the formal or specifying principle of the matter and of the kinds of actions the thing will perform.

see without eyeballs and an optic nerve. But Aquinas argues that conceptual thought—for example understanding what a horse is or what a circle is—is an act that you or I perform but without the use of a bodily organ.

His argument for this last point, very briefly, is that understanding is of a universal nature, but it could not be if the action were performed with a bodily organ (for example, the brain). What we sense—an activity performed with a bodily organ—is always an individual, a *this*. By contrast, what we understand, or grasp in a concept, is universal, a nature held in common by many individuals. We sense this particular color or shape, for example, this magnitude or this water; we understand a nature or essence, for example, what it is to be magnitude or what it is to be water.[9] But if understanding were an act performed with a bodily organ, what it apprehended would have to be a particular since its object would have spatiotemporal dimensions, and it is such dimensions that individualize, that is, make a nature or content to be a *this*, something limited to a particular here and now. So, while sense images are material, and reside in the brain (and so the imagination also is a bodily capacity), intellect or mind is a spiritual power and does not directly make use of a bodily organ.[10]

So in the human being there are actions performed without bodily organs. And from this Aquinas concludes that the human soul is spiritual. His argument is that a thing acts as it is; that is, the character of an action reveals the character of the source of that action. So, since a human being performs actions that are done without bodily organs, without matter, it follows that the formal source of these actions—the human soul—must in some way *be*—exist—independently of matter. That is, since the human being performs spiritual actions, it follows that a part of a human being is spiritual, in the sense of not depending for its existence on matter or bodily parts. This means that the human soul has its actuality or existence through itself, rather than through the actuality of the whole composite, the whole human nature. And so it follows that is the sort of thing that could survive death.[11]

---

9. These were Aristotle's examples: *On the Soul*, book III, chapter 4.

10. A more developed and very clear exposition of this argument: Micheal Augros, *The Immortal in You: How Human Nature Is More Than Science Can Say* (San Francisco: Ignatius, 2017), chapter 5.

11. It also follows that it could not have emerged from lower animals. If the human soul is purely spiritual and its existence is independent of matter, then lower material forces, even acting in concert, are incapable of producing it. Note however that this

This point can be clarified by comparing the human soul with the souls of other animals. Since all of the actions of non-rational animals are physical actions, it follows that such an animal's soul will not have its actuality through itself but will depend for its existence on the whole animal of which it is a part. And so in the case of other animals. Since their soul depends on the existence of the whole animal, when the whole animal ceases to be, their souls also cease to be. However, since the human soul is the formal source of purely spiritual actions, it is independent of matter for its existence. And so when the whole matter-soul composite ceases to be—that is, when death occurs—the human soul does not cease to be.

Thus, the proposal is that, on the one hand, the *human being* is a body-soul composite and so the Platonists or Cartesians are mistaken: I am not a soul that uses a body, the body is part of me. On the other hand, the human *soul* is spiritual, in the sense of being independent of matter for its existence, and survives the death of the whole human being.

The difference between Aquinas's position and the Platonist view is worth underlining. We've seen that Aquinas insists that I am not a soul but a body-soul composite. It must be, Aquinas argues, the same I that understands and wills (spiritual actions), on the one hand, and that walks, breathes, and eats food (material or physical actions), on the other hand. I am one agent, an agent that performs both bodily actions (actions performed with bodily organs) and spiritual actions (actions done without bodily organs). And since what performs bodily actions is a bodily being (again, a thing acts as it is) it follows that the agent that performs bodily actions is a bodily being. But since the agent that is self-conscious and understands—what Platonists and Cartesians identify as the I or the ego—is the same agent as the one that performs bodily actions, it follows that I am a bodily being. The I is not a distinct substance from the body; the body and the soul make up one substance. The soul is a part of a larger whole.[12]

Again, unlike Plato and Descartes, Aquinas insists that the human soul has a natural need for the body in order to perform even its highest operations. That is, even though understanding and willing are purely

---

leaves open the possibility that the organic or bodily aspect of the human being has evolved from lower animals.

12. Aquinas sets out his basic view of the body and the soul in various places. One important and convenient treatment: Thomas Aquinas, *Summa Theologiae*, I, q. 75–76.

spiritual actions, they depend on bodily operations as prerequisites. The human intellect by its very nature depends on sensation as the source of its content for understanding. Aquinas quotes Aristotle, who said that "initially the human intellect is like a black tablet on which nothing is written"—it has no intelligible content innate to it by which to understand. And so it has a natural need for sensation—which of course is a bodily act—to acquire the sensations that provide the data for its understanding.

The intellect's need for sense images (and thus the incompleteness of the mind or spiritual soul) is also shown by the fact that whenever someone wants to understand something, or explain something to others, one adverts to sense images. And if there is an injury or congenital defect in one's brain, then one's ability to understand is diminished. While intellect is not identical to the brain, it naturally depends on it for its data.[13]

So, if these arguments are correct, it follows that the human soul is incapable of performing even its highest operations—understanding and willing—without the cooperation of bodily powers. In other words, even though the acts of intellect and will are themselves purely spiritual actions—that is, actions that are themselves performed without bodily organs—they depend on the products of bodily actions.

In short, the human soul is independent of matter for its existence, but it is designed by nature to be united with a body, to part of a body-soul composite. As a bodily organ, such as a heart, is only a part of a whole because it cannot perform its characteristic function by itself—cannot pump oxygenated blood to other parts of the body without cooperation with other bodily parts—in a similar way the human soul cannot perform its highest actions—understanding and willing—without the cooperation of other parts, especially the brain.[14] And so the human soul is naturally only a part of the larger whole, even though it is independent from the body for its existence.

---

13. Again, to understand something, I need to have an *appropriate* sense image. For example, to understand what a triangle is I need a sense image of a triangular shaped sort rather than of a circular one. This indicates that the sense images do not just trigger one's understanding, but in some way one derives what one understands from sensation. By my intellect I apprehend a content or connection not apprehended by my senses—but I do apprehend it by concentrating on and focusing on what I sense—spiritual things by analogy with material things that are represented to me by sense images. See Thomas Aquinas, *Summa Theologiae*, I, q. 84, art. 6–7.

14. Of course, it is unlike the heart or lung in that it can survive death—does survive death—and is the source of the bodily being, since it is a person.

From these points Aquinas concludes two things about the afterlife of the human soul. From the soul's independence from matter for its existence he concludes that the human soul is naturally immortal. Second, from the fact that it is naturally a part of a larger whole he concludes that when it does survive death it is in an unnatural condition. It is not in accord with the human soul's nature to exist without the body. It calls for union with the body.

What does this position on body and soul imply about human beings during the interim? Again, two points. First, on Aquinas's position there is a significant continuity between what dies, on the one hand, and what is alive after the resurrection, on the other. The death and resurrection of a human being is at least in one respect different from remaking a watch with none of its same components (which it seems would provide only a replica of the original watch). Essential to Aquinas's view is that the human soul is immortal—my soul continues to exist after my death during the interim between my death and my resurrection. When the human being dies, she does cease to be, but a component of her continues. So on Aquinas's view there *is* continuity throughout the duration: before death, after death, and after resurrection—during the whole time the same soul continues to exist.[15] Moreover on his view there is an immanent causal connection between the pre-death human and the post-resurrection human, by way of the soul.[16]

But Aquinas also holds that although the human soul exists during the interim, that soul is not a human being, because a human being is by its nature (or essentially) a matter-form composite. The separated soul is not, of course, a matter-form composite and therefore, he concludes, the separated soul is not a human being.[17] So, Aquinas's view appears also to

---

15. Aquinas also holds that God will reassemble the same matter, or some of the matter at least, that was in the body just before death, and so according to him there also is material continuity. This of course is relevant to the issue being discussed, but the complications it introduces will have to be left for another time. Robert George and I discuss this issue briefly in *Body-Self Dualism and Contemporary Ethical and Political Questions* (New York: Cambridge University Press, 2008), 74–81.

16. An immanent causal connection is that between a reality at one time and that same reality at a subsequent and contiguous time, so that the nature and significant characteristics of the latter are caused by the former. Some argue that the identity of a temporal living being at times t1 and t2 requires an immanent causal connection throughout that time. The immortal soul seems to ensure there is such a connection.

17. Thomas, *Summa Theologiae*, II-II, q. 83, art. 11; *On the Power of God*, q. 9, art. 2.

have a problem of a gap in existence. The soul continues to exist—and so there is continuity—but there is not identity of the person.

III.

So it seems that Aquinas's position still has a gap-in-existence problem. This is not to say that there is no way at all around this difficulty. In fact, Aquinas thinks it is not a fatal difficulty in case of the human being, where the persistence of the soul provides some continuity. Still, it is a difficulty.[18]

But there is a fourth possibility—which I propose as more likely—which is a modification of Aquinas's position. Aquinas holds that the soul survives, but that the human being does not, and that the human being begins to exist again with the resurrection. This position is often called the *corruptionist* position. However, one might hold that the soul survives death, that the soul is incomplete in that it is naturally meant to inform the body, but also that the separated soul is a human being, albeit in a severely injured or debilitated state.[19] The position that the human soul that survives death does qualify as a human being and a human person is often called the *survivalist* position. (The first is called the corruptionist position and the second the survivalist, because on the first the human person ceases to be [corrupts] at death while on the second the human person survives.) I now think that the survivalist position has the better case and that arguments against it can be answered.[20]

Aquinas supports his corruptionist position as follows: what a human being is, is not a soul, but a body-soul composite. Thus, if what exists

---

18. For example, if purgatory is a reality—and I believe it is—then there is at least a *prima facie* problem with one entity—a soul—being purified for the sins committed by another entity—the whole human being. On this point see David Hershenov and Rose Koch-Hershenov, "Personal Identity and Purgatory," *Religious Studies* 42 (2006) 439–51.

19. Debilitated state with respect to what one would be on the level of nature, as it were. If one at that point has the beatific vision—the fullness of direct personal communion with God—then one is in a very blessed condition on the *supernatural* level. Still, on the natural level one is missing something very important, so one is seriously deprived.

20. Some Thomists claim that this was Saint Thomas's position. I think they are wrong on that interpretative issue, but I think the substantive position—the survivalist position—is philosophically and theologically preferable to the other candidate positions.

is only the soul, then that is not a human being. But I don't think that follows. He's right that the human being is not a soul, that a human being is by nature a body-soul composite. Plato and Descartes were wrong; the soul is by its nature a part of a larger whole. But it doesn't follow that I, a human being, could not survive with only one part of me remaining, namely my soul.

The issue, I think, can be clarified by an analogy. Suppose I were a materialist. In that case it would not be incoherent for me to hold that the brain is the indispensable part of me.[21] So I would then say that I am not a brain: right now my brain is only part of me; what I am (I would say) is a thing composed of many material parts and organs, and one very important part—indeed the indispensable part—is the brain. So (if I were a materialist) I would hold that what I am is not a brain, but a complex animal organism.[22] It would still be true that different parts of me could be pruned away—if I got sepsis in my body surgeons might amputate my arms, my legs, and continue. Eventually, I think surgeons might even be able to extract my brain and place it in a vat of nutrients and connect it to tubes to supply it with oxygen and keep it alive (if not presently then perhaps in the future). That brain (or rather, that thing with the brain as its, or my, only remaining part) would then be me, but of course in a highly injured condition. So, in that case I would survive as a brain, even though it would not be true to say that right now I am a brain.

But the logic of what was just said about the brain, from a materialist perspective, applies to the spiritual soul, given that a human being has a spiritual soul. One can hold that a human being can survive as a soul—but that doesn't mean that right now I am a soul. Suppose a human being were pared down to her brain. She would still be alive even though a human being is not essentially a brain (at that point her only remaining part would be her brain). But in truth the paring could (and will) go further so that the only part left is the soul: in that case the only part left is a spiritual component, the soul.[23]

---

21. I do hold that it is the indispensable *material* part of me, or the indispensable part of the organic part of the human being—but let that pass for the moment.

22. Though I am not a materialist, I still think that a human being is an animal organism, but it will be simpler to set that aside for the moment.

23. The position set out here is defended by David Hershenov and Rose Koch-Hershenov, "Personal Identity and Purgatory," 439–51, and Christopher Tollefsen, "Brain Death and Irreplaceable Parts," *Life and Learning XXVI: Proceedings of the 2017 Conference of the University Faculty for Life* (2017), 23–35.

I have said that you and I are not now souls. But even after death when our souls are all that is left of us, we will not—in the strict sense—be souls. The human being will be alive and the human being's only part will be her soul, but being-a-soul is not what she is. When a tree is pared down to a trunk one may say in a loose sense that it is a trunk. But strictly speaking what survives is a tree and its essence is different from what occupied that space before, that is, the trunk. For a trunk is essentially a part of a larger whole; when the tree has been pared down so that the only part of it left is what used to be a trunk (what used to be part of the larger whole), it is now a whole. Since the trunk was not a whole, what exists in the place where a trunk was is no longer a trunk, but a tree occupying the same space that the trunk (the part) previously occupied. If this is true, it does not mean that the human being's essence is to be a soul, à la Plato or Descartes—but only that the soul is the indispensable part of the human being.[24] So, on this approach the human soul survives death and is alive for some duration before the resurrection. During this interim the human being is alive though her only part is the soul. After the resurrection the human being is made whole again, in whatever condition or place (heaven, hell, or purgatory) that human being then lives.

IV.

In this last section I want to examine the connection between the body-soul issue and our notion of heaven.[25] The body-soul question is crucial

---

24. One might object: a human being is essentially an animal—a rational animal but an animal nonetheless. But during the interim, when only the soul survives, what is alive is not an animal, not a sentient organism (which is the definition of an animal). Reply: what exists was designed to and oriented to sensing, nourishing itself, functioning by metabolism, etc., as well as understanding and willing. So it fits the definition of *animal*. True, it does not now have the organs needed to perform actions such as sensing and nourishment. But it is internally oriented to being united and participating in such bodily actions. That seems to me sufficient for fitting the definition and thus continuing to be an animal—though this is admittedly a peculiar instance. On this definition of "animal" see: Allison Krile Thornton, "Varieties of Animalism," *Philosophy Compass* 11 (2016) 515–26; Jason Eberl, *The Nature of Human Persons* (Notre Dame: University of Notre Dame Press, forthcoming), chapter 7.

25. I should also mention that there are several ethical issues where the fact that human beings are bodily beings is important. If a human being is body as soul then it makes sense that the human body has inherent, rather than instrumental, significance. This point is important for ethical questions about the beginning of life, the end of life, and sex and marriage.

also for our notion of heaven, especially the point that we are body-soul composites, not just souls possessing bodies.

There is a scene in the 1989 film *Field of Dreams* that, I think, helps illustrate the point I want to make. This film, which starred Kevin Costner, James Earl Jones, and others, touched on the question of what heaven is. In the movie, Kevin Costner plays the character Ray Kinsella, a farmer in Iowa, who has a lovely wife and beautiful little daughter, and is working hard to keep their farm and make ends meet. About fifteen years before, Ray had had a falling out with his father and left home, even refusing at one point to play catch with his dad, who had been an avid baseball fan and a minor league baseball player in his own time. That had been just a short time before his dad's death.

The high point of the movie comes near the end when Ray is reunited with his dad, who is mysteriously allowed to return and play baseball with other dead baseball players on Ray's farm. Ray introduces his dad to his wife and daughter. Afterward, when they are talking alone, Ray's dad asks him, "Can I ask you something? Is this heaven?" Ray replies that, no, this is Iowa, and his dad says, "I could have sworn this is heaven." A little later in the same conversation they come back to the subject. They both look back at the farmhouse where Ray's wife and daughter are sitting on the swing on the front porch, and this time Ray says, "Yes, I guess this *is* heaven." And then—the last dialogue of the movie—Ray asks his dad, his voice crackling, "Dad, you want to play catch?" and his dad says, "Yes, I'd like that," and the movie ends showing Ray and his dad playing catch.

Now the movie's answer about what heaven is isn't quite right. When Ray says, "Yes, I guess this *is* heaven," he is no doubt referring to the home and the love and the family that he is blessed with on his Iowa farm, also no doubt including his reconciliation with his dad. But that's not entirely right. Heaven is much *more* than that. Heaven will include a supernatural, intimate personal communion with God, our heavenly Father, a mysterious and intimate sharing in the triune life of Father, Son and Holy Spirit. As Saint Paul says, "Eye has not seen, ear has not heard what the Lord has prepared for those who love him" (1 Cor 2:9). So, heaven is more than human love and family. But the movie is not entirely wrong either: Heaven will *include* what they see when looking back at the farmhouse and Ray's wife and daughter. Heaven will *include* created love and family; it will include the human relationships and all of the natural goods that we help, with God's grace, to build up. Heaven will include our relationships to all our friends, and no doubt also baseball and farms and swings and porches.

Heaven will centrally include communion with God, a mysterious sharing in his own divine life—but that is *supernatural*. We have every reason to believe that heaven will include *both* supernatural fulfillment *and* natural or human fulfillment as well. And so if we are bodily beings—if the body is part of what each of us is—then heaven will not be a purely spiritual reality. It will be spiritual, but it will also include bodily fulfillment—bodily life and health, playing catch with your dad, doing things together with your mom and dad, brothers and sisters and all sorts of friends—it will include all of the good relationships that are embodied and built up by our doing things together.

This is an important point. Often people think of heaven as if it were purely spiritual—with the result that it may seem so alien to our experience that heaven becomes less appealing than it should be.[26]

The idea that heaven is purely spiritual has also elicited an important secularist objection to religion, the objection articulated by various critics of Christianity such as Nietzsche, Marx, Freud and others. These thinkers object that concern for heaven detracts from concern for real problems in this world. Religion, and in particular Christianity, they argue, views this world as a mere means in relation to the next, and views the temporal as merely instrumentally valuable. And therefore, the objection concludes, religion denigrates the temporal and bodily goods such as health and this-worldly relationships.

The answer to this objection is that it wrongly assumes that according to Christianity the temporal and the eternal, the material and the spiritual, are in fundamental conflict, so that valuing or devoting oneself to one requires completely devaluing the other. But that is not Christian teaching. Devoting oneself to heaven (seeking first the kingdom) does not detract from one's respect and concern for genuine natural and bodily goods, since heaven includes both supernatural and natural goods, and both spiritual and bodily goods. Heaven, the kingdom of God, is not a purely spiritual reality. In the end, in the fulfillment of his plan, God will "unite all things in Christ, things in heaven and things on earth" (Eph

---

26. On the importance of an inclusive view of heaven see Germain Grisez, *The Way of the Lord Jesus, Volume 1: Christian Moral Principles* (Chicago: Franciscan Herald, 1983), chapters 19 and 34.

1:10; cf. Col 1:19–20). Heaven will be a community of divine and created persons, richly sharing in both divine life and created goods.[27]

I have examined how questions about what a human being is arise in the context of thinking about the resurrection and about heaven. There is a puzzle about how a human being could be dead at one time but numerically the same human individual alive at some later time. We have examined some of the pros and cons for different views on that issue, including Platonism, materialism, and Thomism. I have suggested that on this question a modified version of Thomas Aquinas's position on the body and the soul has much to commend it. I also briefly argued that this position (or something like it) on the body and the soul fits what is revealed to us about heaven and the relationship between this life and heaven.

---

27. Grisez, *Way of the Lord Jesus*, chapter 34.

6

On Dying

Gilbert Meilaender

In Felix Salten's *Bambi*, a book that happens to be a favorite of mine, there is a chapter which consists entirely of a conversation between two leaves that are clinging precariously to a tree. Here is a part of their exchange:

> They were silent for a while. Then the first leaf said quietly to herself, "Why must we fall? . . ."
> The second leaf asked
> "What happens to us when we have fallen?"
> "We sink down . . ."
> "What is under us?"
> The first leaf answered,
> "I don't know, some say one thing, some another, but nobody knows."
> The second leaf asked,
> "Do we feel anything, do we know anything about ourselves when we're down there?"
> The first leaf answered,
> "Who knows? Not one of all those down there has ever come back to tell us about it." . . .
> "Let's remember how beautiful it was, how wonderful, when the sun came out and shone so warmly that we thought we'd burst with life. Do you remember? And the morning dew, and the mild and splendid nights . . . ."
> A moist wind blew, cold and hostile, through the tree-tops.

"Ah, now," said the second leaf, "I . . ." Then her voice broke off.
She was torn from her place and spun down.
Winter had come.[1]

If that is where we human beings also find ourselves when thinking about death, as a mystery beyond our ken, it should be no surprise that many in our culture have concluded that we should try to master it. And so, we want to live for as long as we can, with as much health and vigor as we can, enjoying that warm sunshine, morning dew, and splendid nights. To be healthy octogenarians (or better!) is fine with us. What we do not want is decline and frailty; we do not want to find ourselves clinging weakly to the tree of life. Our ideal is to live with health and strength for as long as we can—and then one day just fall off the cliff.

Since, however, our future may be more like that of one of those leaves clinging to the tree, blown by a cold and hostile wind, many among us seek a way to control our ending. We begin to think that perhaps we should propel ourselves over the cliff or find a friend who will give us a gentle push. And so, our culture—and, indeed, much of Western culture more generally—has begun to look with favor on suicide, assisted suicide, and euthanasia as choice-worthy ways to meet our end. And if not one of those down there has ever come back to tell us about it, there may be nothing foolish about such an attitude.

But there are also some of us who believe that one has come back to tell us about death and that in Jesus we see the true master of death. To enter into his story is to begin to see our life and death differently—to see it within the history of redemption. All things were made through him, John's Gospel says. The long, slow story of God's election of Israel moves toward him, the faithful and obedient Israelite. And he promises to be with us—in all his mastery of death—even to the end of the age. To come to terms with dying, therefore, to think about what holy dying might mean, we must, as Karl Barth put it, "accompany this history of God and man from creation to reconciliation and redemption, indicating the mystery of the encounter at each point on the path according to its own distinctive character."[2]

We have, then, three angles of vision from which to ponder the meaning of our dying. Because we are God's creatures, there must be some account of life that accepts, honors, and celebrates the limits of our

---

1. Felix Salten, *Bambi* (New York: Grosset & Dunlap, 1929), 11–15.
2. Karl Barth, *Church Dogmatics* (Edinburgh: T. & T. Clark, 1961), III/4:26.

finitude and the time we are allotted. Because we are sinners whom God has in Jesus acted to reconcile, our life moves toward death and is disordered in countless ways that come under God's judgment. And because we are heirs of the redeemed future God has promised in the risen Jesus, because he knows us by name, we are promised that one day we will come to share in the life eternal that Father, Son, and Spirit live. I want to think about our dying within these three angles of vision afforded us by the history of redemption, prefacing each of the three with a stanza from a hymn by a nineteenth-century Norwegian pastor, Magnus Langstad. The hymn is "I Know of a Sleep in Jesus' Name."[3]

Created Life

> I know of a peaceful eventide;
> And when I am faint and weary,
> At times with the journey sorely tried,
> Thro' hours that are long and dreary.
> Then often I yearn to lay me down
> And sink into blissful slumber.

We are not meant to live this created life forever, and that for two reasons. The first has to do with understanding and honoring the finite character of our life.

Even when things go well for us, the life we live has a natural trajectory that begins in growth and development but moves, eventually, toward decline and death. No doubt this saddens us, but, when death does not come prematurely due to illness or injury, it is not simply an evil. For, after all, it is the nature of finite, organic life. Generally, and quite properly, we refer to created life as a gift from God. But it is also a task. Staying alive is work, the work we call metabolism. In a complicated process of exchange we take in the oxygen that our cells use to create the energy living organisms need, and we release carbon dioxide back into the environment. And this task will finally defeat each of us.

A living human being is not just a thing, not an inanimate object. We are living organisms, bodies animated by soul. We do not exist the way a rock does, "simply and fixedly what it is, identical with itself over

---

3. I will use the translation of this hymn from *The Lutheran Hymnal* of 1941.

time, and with no need to maintain that identity by anything else it does."[4] Rather, constantly hovering between being and non-being, we experience life as a fragile gift, difficult to sustain, filled with beauties that do not last. And when a day comes when we can no longer carry out the work metabolism involves, we become things: the inanimate objects we call corpses. It seems right to me, therefore, that the last words of my paternal grandfather were simply, "*Ich kann nicht mehr.*" I can't any longer.

This does not make our allotted time any less a gift; it simply characterizes the kind of gift it is. Not God's timeless eternity, but a life fit for one who is creature, not Creator. This explains why we can hardly help but approve when Odysseus, offered the choice between an immortal life with the nymph Calypso and a return home to his wife Penelope, chooses to return. He chooses, that is, to be not a god but a man, accepting a life that is strictly on loan, always fragile, and moving inevitably toward death. That is the nature of our allotted time in which, sooner or later, we grow, as the hymn says, "faint and weary."

But there is also a second reason we are not meant to live this created life forever. The very same metabolic exchanges that mark our finitude point to something else: to a freedom that transcends earthly life. For we do not simply persist unchangingly over time the way an inanimate rock does. On the contrary, it is by undergoing constant change that we persist over time, and we somehow both are and are not the same person through all those changes. Drop me from the top of a fifty-story building, and something happens in my fall that is different from the fall of a rock. For I know myself as a falling object, which means that I can in some way distance myself from that object. I am that falling object, but I am also not simply equated with it.

Our being is ecstatic. That is to say, we have a kind of inner freedom from our own substance. In that freedom we reach out for something more, longing for what Augustine called "beauty so ancient and so new."[5] It is, of course, possible to stifle—or try to stifle—this longing, as Augustine also well knew. Both Epicureans and Stoics, in their different ways, held that we need not fear death. For, as they said, if what awaits us is oblivion, there will be neither sensation nor misery to experience. But their argument ignores one thing: in oblivion, the thirst Augustine

---

4. Hans Jonas, "The Burden and Blessing of Mortality," *Hastings Center Report* 22.1 (1992), 34–40, esp. 35.

5. Augustine, *The Confessions of Saint Augustine*, translated by Rex Warner (New York: Signet Classics, 2001), 10.27.

believed characterizes our created life will never have been quenched; we will not have found that "beauty so ancient and so new." This created life will turn out to have been a futile absurdity—marked by a longing that is never to be answered or satisfied.

The deepest desire of our hearts, a desire implanted in us at the creation, is not simply for quantitatively more of this life, lovely as it often is. Augustine had it right. We desire a beauty that is qualitatively different, not given in ordinary experience. To be sure, this created life is filled with sights and sounds of great beauty, and it is right that our hearts should be drawn to them. Desire for longer life and grief at the death of loved ones is surely not wrong, not even when we believe that the one whom we loved has arrived at a "peaceful eventide" and a "blissful slumber." Nevertheless, as a character in Wallace Stegner's novel *The Spectator Bird* says, "A reasonably endowed, reasonably well-intentioned man can walk through the world's great kitchen from end to end and arrive at the back door hungry."[6]

From two different angles, therefore, we might say that we are not meant to live this created life forever. As organisms, animated bodies, we discover that decline and death are built into the trajectory of our lives. As thirsty creatures, thirsting for God, we may come to see that more of this life could never satisfy our desire for something qualitatively different. Taking these two truths seriously can help us when we think about our dying. We have received this life as a gift; if we seek to master it by deliberately ending our life (with or without another's help), we fail to honor the gift, and we may miss the way in which it calls us out of ourselves to the Giver. And we have received this life as a task; to live worthily is to take up that task for as many years as God gives us.

Still, we do not have to do everything in our power to stay alive, as if the longest life possible were always the one required of us. That is why we can admire the kind of soldiers described by J. Glenn Gray in his classic work, *The Warriors*—soldiers who "do not desire to live forever, for they feel that this would be a sacrifice of quality to gain quantity." In their willingness to lose their life in a good cause they are, he writes, "affirming human finiteness and limitation as a morally desirable fact."[7] Likewise, when each of us does battle with illness and suffering, we are not required to use whatever medical treatments offer the longest life. Sometimes, for

---

6. Wallace Stegner, *The Spectator Bird* (Garden City, NY: Doubleday, 1976), 69.

7. J. Glenn Gray, *The Warriors: Reflections on Men in Battle* (New York, Evanston: Harper Torchbooks, 1967), 122.

some of us, a life which, though shorter, is free of treatments that are of little benefit or are excessively burdensome, may well be the right choice. That is not an attempt at mastery; it is simply accepting the truth that the gift of this life, lovely as it can be, is not meant to satisfy the deepest desire of the human heart.

Eventually, therefore, unable to sustain the task earthly life sets before us, and reaching toward One whose beauty surpasses every created good, we will come "faint and weary" to "eventide," yearning to "sink into blissful slumber." That is the shape of our created life.

Reconciled Life

> O Jesus, draw near my dying bed
> And take me into Thy keeping
> And say when my spirit hence is fled,
> "This child is not dead, but sleeping."
> And leave me not, Savior, till I rise
> To praise Thee in life eternal.

Once we appreciate those two truths about created life, we might, of course, even while free of any Stoic desire for mastery, come to believe that death is no great evil for us. Certainly, many sincere Christians have sometimes thought that way. Thus, for example, William Law, in his classic *Serious Call to a Devout and Holy Life*, places in the mouth of Penitens, an earnest believer near death, this sentiment: "For what is there miserable or dreadful in death, but the consequences of it? . . . If I am now going into the joys of God, could there be any reason to grieve?"[8] If, however, we are drawn to such a view, we will have to find a way to come to terms with Saint Paul, who characterizes death as both the wages of sin and the last enemy.[9] What would it mean to take him seriously?

We can make a beginning by returning to the truth that our being is ecstatic, that as self-transcending beings we have a kind of freedom from our own substance. In describing created life, I found in that self-transcendence a hint that our desire was for a Beauty never fully experienced in this life—and, hence, that earthly life is not meant to last forever. But

---

8. William Law, *A Serious Call to a Devout and Holy Life: The Spirit of Love*, The Classics of Western Spirituality (New York: Paulist, 1978), 70.

9. Rom 6:23; 1 Cor 15:26.

perhaps the ecstatic quality of human beings can teach us another truth as well—namely, that each person's death is not just an instance of the course of human life but is a unique occurrence.

For *my* death, or *your* death, is not only or merely a participation in something universal, something common to all created beings. My death is also unique, a one-time event—as is yours. There is no replacing us when we are gone. That is the point of one of Tolstoy's most quoted passages in *The Death of Ivan Ilyich*. Moving toward death, Ivan ponders the existential strangeness of the common syllogism: All men are mortal, Caius is a man; therefore Caius is mortal. This, he reflects, "had always seemed to him correct as applied to Caius, but by no means to himself. That man Caius represented man in the abstract, and so the reasoning was perfectly sound; but he was not Caius, not an abstract man."[10] Thus, what Ivan, without batting an eye, can serenely say of Caius—that he is not meant to live this earthly life forever—has an altogether different ring when he says it of himself. His life is not just an instance of the general shape of human life. No, he had a particular mother and father, particular childhood experiences, particular loves, a particular vocation—and, most of all, self-awareness. Awareness of himself as the absolutely unrepeatable and non-interchangeable person: Ivan Ilyich.

"The point of a proper name," Ralph McInerny once wrote,

> is that it [is] not common to many, and yet many people do bear identical names. . . . But even when two persons have the same proper name it does not become a common noun, like "man." All the John Smiths that have been, are, and will be have nothing in common but the name; it does not name something common to them all. There is an inescapable nominalism here. God calls us all by our proper name, and He is unlikely to confuse one John Smith with another.[11]

It is hard, then, to experience my death, that one-time event, as merely an instance of a natural occurrence toward which all human lives move. Indeed, I am almost tempted to say that we deceive ourselves if we try to experience it only in that way.

From this perspective it is not so much that I move toward death as that it moves toward me. It comes as judgment. We may say that one who

---

10. Leo Tolstoy, *The Death of Ivan Ilyich* (New York: Bantam, 1981), 79.

11. Ralph McInerny, *I Alone Have Escaped to Tell You: My Life and Pastimes* (Notre Dame: University of Notre Dame Press, 2006), 162.

dies has "passed" or "passed away," but those perhaps comforting formulations do not uncover the full meaning of a person's dying. One who dies has been summoned—summoned for judgment. Jaroslav Pelikan noted that Cyprian—Bishop of Carthage in the mid-third century—seems to have been the first Latin writer to use the word *arcessitio* ("summons") to refer to death. "To Cyprian," Pelikan writes, "the idea of the summons connotes the authority of the Supreme Judge to order a man into his presence and to demand an account from him of all that he has been and done." This is no gentle "passing," the kind of event that could hardly be said to call our very being into question. No, death so understood moves toward us as encounter, as "the irresistible call of the Summoner."[12] If we have learned to hear in death the voice of the holy God summoning us, might we not come to see the vanity of our attempts to master and control our dying?

Still more, must we not learn to pray, "O Jesus, draw near my dying bed, / And take me into thy keeping"? We can reconcile ourselves to the thought of being summoned for judgment only as we learn to look to the One whom Karl Barth so aptly characterized as "the judge judged in our place."[13] If, as Ivan Ilyich came to realize, each of us dies a death that is uniquely his own, then each of us is, as Ralph McInerny observed, a non-interchangeable child of God whom God knows by name. Recalling his own brush with death, Richard John Neuhaus called to mind Potter's Field on Hart Island in New York City. In that field for roughly two centuries there have been buried, in simple numbered boxes, thousands of unclaimed corpses. And in the middle of the field stands a large stone inscribed with the words, "He Knows Them by Name."[14]

This is especially important for us to underscore when we think of those who have died or will die prematurely—as we say from the perspective of our finite created life. Although they have not lived what we are pleased to call a full life, we dare not make that the basis for any judgment about the worth and meaning of their lives. That judgment is not ours to make. For, in fact, in every moment of life, short or long, we are equidistant from God.

---

12. Jaroslav Pelikan, *The Shape of Death: Life, Death, and Immortality in the Early Fathers* (New York: Abingdon, 1961), 69.

13. Karl Barth, *Church Dogmatics* (Edinburgh: T. & T. Clark, 1956), IV/1:211-83.

14. Richard John Neuhaus, *As I Lay Dying: Meditations upon Returning* (New York: Basic Books, 2002), 60.

In Westwood Cemetery in Oberlin, Ohio, in an area of the cemetery known as Missionary Rest, a marker at the gravesite of one of the children of an Oberlin missionary reads:

> Dear Jesus
> You know that I love you
> Take me to yourself.

That gets it exactly right. The days or weeks of a child who dies soon after (or even before) birth are not only days of a life tragically cut short, though of course they are that from the perspective of the normal trajectory of created life. They are also the days or weeks of a God-aimed spirit, whose every moment is lived before One for whom a thousand years are but as yesterday when it is past. Surely Jesus, the Child of Mary, will draw near their dying bed as he will ours.

The One who summons each of us as death moves toward us, the One who summons us for judgment, is One with the power and authority to say, "This child is not dead, but sleeping." To be sure, as the Letter to the Hebrews reminds us, it is "a fearful thing to fall into the hands of the living God."[15] But when that living God is the judge judged in our place, then, as Barth says, we "fall into *His* hands and not the hands of another."[16]

Redeemed Life

> I know of a morning bright and fair
> When tidings of joy shall wake us,
> When songs from on high shall fill the air
> And God to his glory take us.
> When Jesus shall bid us rise from sleep,
> How joyous that hour of waking.

When we turn now to think about the meaning of our dying in relation to the redeemed life we are promised, we are, of course, pretty much on our own. As C. S. Lewis once put it in a passage often quoted, "Our present outlook might be like that of a small boy who, on being told that the sexual act was the highest bodily pleasure, should immediately ask whether

---

15. Heb 10:31.
16. Karl Barth, *Church Dogmatics* (Edinburgh: T. & T. Clark, 1960), III/2:609.

you ate chocolates at the same time.... The boy knows chocolate: he does not know the positive thing that excludes it."[17]

One thing we can say with some assurance is that the promised life of the redeemed creation begins to mark us even now, as we live toward our death. "If any one is in Christ, he is [present tense] a new creation," St. Paul writes, enunciating in his own idiom the Johannine teaching that to know Jesus is life eternal.[18] Therefore, in his *Small Catechism* Luther describes baptism as signifying "that the old Adam in us with all sins and evil desires is to be drowned and die through daily contrition and repentance, and on the other hand that daily a new man is to come forth and rise up to live before God in righteousness and purity forever."[19] Hence, the death toward which we move—or which moves toward us—is the last gasp of a life the Holy Spirit has been putting to death in us since our baptism, and the redeemed life that will one day be fully realized in us is already present in our life here and now.

When that last dying gasp comes, it will not come as a fulfillment or even just as a natural development of the life that has preceded it. It will come as the advent of God's promised future. As Moltmann observed, it will arrive not as *futurum*, a development that draws out potential already present, but as *adventus*, which comes to us as something new.[20] Moltmann makes the point nicely with reference to Revelation 1:4, which reads: "Grace to you and peace from him who is and who was and who is to come." We might, Moltmann notes, expect a slightly different formula: "him who is and who was and who will be." But the verse speaks not of the one who will be as he has been in the past but of the one who is to come.[21] And if that is the right way to think about the coming of the promised redeemed creation, we see from yet another angle what folly it would be to suppose that we should try to control or master our dying. Instead, we want to learn to live in hope, a virtue that specifically excludes mastery.

---

17. C. S. Lewis, *Miracles: A Preliminary Study* (New York: Macmillan, 1947), 153.

18. 2 Cor 5:17; John 17:3.

19. Robert Kolb and Timothy J. Wengert, eds., *The Book of Concord: The Confessions of the Evangelical Lutheran Church* (Minneapolis: Fortress, 2000), 360. Translation slightly revised.

20. Jürgen Moltmann, *The Coming of God: Christian Eschatology* (Minneapolis: Fortress, 1996), 25.

21. Moltmann, *Coming of God*, 23.

To be sure, if the creation is to be redeemed, the promised future for which we hope must in some way be a restoration of the world we have corrupted. So when that promised future breaks into our world at Easter, we are, on the one hand, helped to honor "the beauty and order of the life that was the creator's gift to his creation and is restored there." But, on the other hand, we are also turned "from the empty tomb" to live toward "a new moment of participation in God's work and being."[22]

For what exactly, then, do we hope? This is by no means an easy question to answer. Surely, we hope to rest in the peace of Jesus, to be taken into an ever-deepening participation in the life of love that is the Triune God. But what can that mean? I have already said that we are pretty much on our own when it comes to being more precise here. Pretty much, but not entirely. For, after all, one has come back to tell us about it. This must, at least, mean that we hope not for an escape from the body but for a renewed and transformed life in the body.

To be sure, it comes rather naturally to us to think simply in terms of a continued existence of the soul apart from the body. Contrasting an inner and outer self does capture something true to our lived experience. For as surely as I know that the component parts of my body are being constantly replaced throughout life, I also have a sense that in, with, and under that constant change *I* somehow persist. Nevertheless, if a human person is the *union* of soul and body, the prospect of a dissolution of the body while the soul lives on untouched could hardly be comforting. For that would mean that our death was essentially "the *threat* of a bodiless life," and it would make almost inexplicable Christian hope for the resurrection of the body.[23] What we can and should say, however, is that, although those who have died in Christ may be "away from the body," as Saint Paul says, they are "at home with the Lord."[24] And because the Lord with whom they are at home is the resurrected Christ, the Living One, they too must somehow live in him. Quite rightly, therefore, even now as we live in hope, we offer our praise week after week in the Eucharist "with Angels and Archangels, and with all the company of heaven."

As we live toward our dying, or await its summons to claim us, we must therefore honor with Christian burial the bodies of those who have died in the faith. Unless we are among those still living when the risen

---

22. Oliver O'Donovan, *Self, World, and Time* (Grand Rapids: Eerdmans, 2013), 92.
23. Barth, *Church Dogmatics*, III/2, 352. Emphasis added.
24. 2 Cor 5:9.

Lord returns in glory, we must all make our way to that day through death. And it is in the funeral service, the rite of Christian burial, that we honor to the end the gift of created life, a life the incarnate Son of God has shared with us and has promised to redeem. The meaning of that service is, however, increasingly obscured in our world. Simply put, Christians should do what the title of Thomas Long's book-length discussion of the Christian funeral urges: *Accompany Them with Singing*.[25]

A Christian funeral is not a memorial service, not a celebration of life, not an occasion for eulogizing the deceased—any and all of which can be and often are done without the presence of a dead body. In the words of Thomas Lynch, the mortician-essayist: "A good funeral transports the newly deceased and the newly bereaved to the borders of a changed reality. The dead are disposed of in a way that says they mattered to us, and the living are brought to the edge of a life they will lead without the one who has died. We deal with death by dealing with the dead, not just the idea but also the sad and actual fact of the matter—the dead body."[26] After all, the entire Christian life is a pilgrimage, a journey that begins in baptism and moves toward the new creation which the risen Christ now lives and promises will be ours. We who have accompanied a newly deceased person along this way, and certainly those of us who have been loved ones and fellow believers, ought not to cut the journey short. The funeral gives expression not to our mastery of death but to our hope for the promised redemption.

There are, moreover, reasons to think that, although cremation of the dead body is not in itself wrong, burial in the ground is likely to capture better the Christian significance of death. The absence of a corpse may easily suggest that the body is not the place of the person's presence—not the kernel, but simply a dispensable husk. Yet, as Saint Paul writes, the dead body "is sown in weakness, it is raised in power. It is sown a physical body, it is raised a spiritual body."[27] And so we place the bodies of our dead in the ground, in the hope that God in his own time will give them new life.

For now, then, we need not try to master death, for we know that it has been mastered. Until the day comes when others must lay us in the ground, we give thanks for the beauties of created life, we try to prepare

---

25. Thomas G. Long, *Accompany Them with Singing—The Christian Funeral* (Louisville: Westminster John Knox Press, 2009).

26. Thomas Lynch, "Good Grief," *Christian Century*, July 26, 2003, 20.

27. 1 Cor 15:43–44.

ourselves for the summons that must one day come, and we wait in hope for the promised day of resurrection. If we, like so many before us, die before that day comes, we will rest in the peace of Jesus, trusting that on "a morning bright and fair" he will "bid us rise from sleep" to share with all who hope in him that joyous "hour of waking."

7

What Is the Relationship of the Brain, Consciousness, and Christian Faith?

Nancey Murphy

Introduction

GIVEN THAT THE GENERAL topic of this volume is the good for humanity, it would seem that we first need an answer to the question of what humans, most basically, are. Yet, there are a surprising number of conflicting views, often unacknowledged, in our society. One very important type is found in Patrick Lee's chapter;[1] this is one I would call a version of holistic dualism, meaning that a human is essentially body and soul. However, there is another version of dualism that takes the soul alone to be essential. The church has, for centuries, favored the former and rejected the latter.

I have been asked to represent the view, which I and many others argue is equally acceptable for Christians, of what at this point I will call non-reductive physicalism. That is, a human is not made up of two substances but only one, and yet we are not mere animals; we have all the capacities that have regularly been attributed to a non-material substance.

---

1. In this volume, chapter 5.

Given Lee's advocacy of Thomas Aquinas's work to provide what many would call a dualist account, it may appear that I am being wicked to use Thomas myself to argue against dualism. However, I do this often because Thomas provides what I believe is the most insightful account of human capacities, which can just as well be seen as attributes provided by our complex neural systems along with our embeddedness in highly developed cultures. This physicalist position also has an unacceptable competitor in our culture: reductive physicalism. Therefore, I might better have titled my chapter "Brains, Reductionism, and Christian Faith."

Because holistic dualism has been the most prominent Christian teaching in the church over the course of approximately seventeen centuries, I will begin, first, by briefly giving my reasons for arguing that the Bible does not teach dualism, and that it only began to appear as Christianity moved from a largely Hebraic setting farther into the Hellenistic world. Next, I will give a short sampling of the ways in which biology and neuroscience are finding explanations for capacities that Thomas attributed to the soul. However, I will add a section specifically on the concept of the will and its role in ethics and theology, beginning with contemporary Thomist philosopher Alasdair MacIntyre's account of morality, but then adding a cognitive-neuroscience analysis to his philosophical theory. Before addressing morality, though, it will be necessary to provide an argument for the defeat of causal reductionism.

Why Christians Do Not Need Dualism

To put it in oversimplified terms, Christian scholars came to a near consensus by the 1950s on rejecting dualism; biblical scholars and theologians had judged that body-soul dualism was not a part of original Christian teaching, and ought to be rejected as a Greek cultural accretion. This is an oversimplification in several ways. First, Protestant scholarship in the United States has been sharply divided between conservative and liberal. The debates in Germany and Britain regarding biblical concepts of human nature and life after death were taken up by liberal scholars in the United States at the same time. Only now are similar issues being debated by conservative Protestants. Second, the dynamics in Catholic theology and biblical studies are more complex; however, I hazard a guess that Catholic biblical scholars are more likely than theologians to reject dualism.² Finally, whatever was decided in liberal seminaries and universities seventy years ago, it apparently never leaked out to the churches. When I poll audiences in the United States, I find that the vast majority are either body-soul dualists or hold a tripartite view of humans as body, soul, and spirit.

If, as I claim, Christians have been wrong for so long in taking the Bible to teach dualism, this needs an explanation. The first issue that arose was whether body-soul dualism was the teaching of the Old Testament. This was raised by H. Wheeler Robinson in 1911.³ It is now recognized by nearly all scholars that there is no dualism in the Old Testament. The reason that Christians could so easily read it dualistically was that the Old Testament was translated into Greek. The result is called the Septuagint, completed around 250 BCE. Thus, Greek anthropological terms were used to translate Hebrew terms. For example, the Greek word *psyche* was used to translate the Hebrew *nephesh*; *pneuma* was used to translate *ruach*. Later Christians then read them in light of their meanings in Greek philosophy, and have translated them accordingly into modern languages as soul and spirit respectively.

But then we might ask why contemporary scholars believe that the Septuagint used what we now see to be inappropriate word choices for Hebraic anthropological terms. Biblical scholar James Dunn offers a compelling explanation. He distinguishes what he calls "aspective" and "partitive" accounts of human nature. Greek philosophers tended to ask, what are the essential *parts* that make up a human being? In contrast, biblical authors were interested in an *aspective* account. Here each term stands for the whole person thought of from a certain angle. For example, Paul's distinction between spirit and flesh is not the later distinction between soul and body. Paul was speaking of two ways of living: one in conformity with the Spirit of God, and the other in conformity with concerns of the world, many of which involved family, kinship, and ethnicity—hence the world of the flesh.⁴

In addition, the development of dualism in Christianity can be rather precisely dated. For example, Clement of Rome, writing around the

---

2. For a more complete account see Nancey Murphy, *Bodies and Souls, or Spirited Bodies?* (Cambridge: Cambridge University Press, 2006).

3. H. Wheeler Robinson, *The Christian Doctrine of Man* (Edinburgh: T. & T. Clark, 1991).

4. James G. D. Dunn, *The Theology of Paul the Apostle* (Grand Rapids: Eerdmans, 1998), 54.

year 95, used the word "immortality" but taught that it is a gift from God due to the resurrection of the body, with no mention of a soul. The fate of those who were not saved was simply death.[5] Polycarp, bishop of Smyrna until the year 155, described humans in terms of body and soul, but did not believe the soul to be immortal; he gave thanks at his martyrdom for the fact that he would have a part in "the resurrection of eternal life, both of soul and body."[6] Views such as Polycarp's "conditional immortality" of the soul, versus Greek-influenced views of an innately immortal soul existed side by side from near the end of the second century, for example, held by Athenagoras (d. 190) until Augustine's day (d. 430).[7]

While these disagreements about human nature continue, there is widespread agreement that Jesus preached about the establishment of the kingdom of God, not about souls going to heaven. And bodily resurrection is the proper New Testament hope for eternal life.

Contributions from Neuroscience

As noted in my introduction, it may appear to be an *ad hominem* move to use Thomas's account of the soul to argue for physicalism, but it provides the best account I have found in Christian thought of human capacities—or, in line with Dunn, of the assorted *aspects* of human nature.

Thomas, following ancient philosopher Aristotle, attributed souls to plants and animals. The human soul is tripartite, incorporating all the capacities of both plant and animal souls, as well as our own particular rational soul. The vegetative soul, in the first instance, is simply the life principle.[8] The question of what makes something alive is now handled by biology.

Many biologists today write that the minimum requirements for life are self-maintenance, growth, and reproduction. Thus, a sphere of proteins and other large molecules is living if it has a membrane separating it from its environment; the membrane is permeable enough to allow for intake of nutrients; it has the ability to repair itself if damaged; and finally,

---

5. Le Roy Edwin Froom, *The Conditionalist Faith of Our Fathers: The Conflict of the Ages Over the Nature and Destiny of Man*, 2 vols. (Washington, DC: Review and Herald, 1966), 1:762–64.

6. Froom, *Conditionalist Faith of Our Fathers*, 791, 795.

7. Froom, *Conditionalist Faith of Our Fathers*, 929.

8. Timothy McDermott, *St Thomas Aquinas Summa Theologia: A Concise Translation* (Westminster, MD: Christian Classics, 1989), 105.

the ability to reproduce, even if only by splitting into two spheres, each of which grows large enough to split again. The three functions Thomas attributed to the vegetative soul were growth, nutrition, and reproduction. The one feature he failed to note was self-repair.

The physicalist thesis is that as we go up the hierarchy of increasingly complex organisms, the other capacities once attributed to the soul will also turn out to be products of complex organization, rather than properties of a non-material entity.

The faculties Thomas attributed to the sensitive soul were locomotion, appetite, emotion, and sensations of two types—the five external senses and what he called "internal senses."[9] I have space to consider only a few these.

A great deal of research has been done on the role of the brain in sense perception. For example, visual perception in higher animals developed from single, light-sensitive cells in primitive organisms. In humans, signals are transmitted from light-sensitive cells in the retina, through a series of processors, to the visual cortex. The striking difference between lower and higher animals is that while the lower ones can respond to stimuli in their environments, they do so without knowing what they are doing; they lack consciousness.

There is a phenomenon called blindsight that helps clarify the difference between conscious and non-conscious perception. Certain victims of damage to the visual cortex are either completely blind or have blind spots in their visual fields. Nonetheless, they are receiving information about their environments. If they are asked to say where an object is they will say that they do not know, but if told to reach for it they do much better than would be expected by chance.[10] So the value of consciousness is that we not only know things about our environment, but we also know that we know. *How* consciousness arises from brain function is, as neuroscientists say, the hard problem. Since experts still do not agree on how this happens, I believe it best to skip over it.[11]

Thomas's four interior senses are particularly interesting in that they show his skill as a cognitive scientist and also link up with quite detailed work in neuroscience. These are attributes shared with higher animals. Here is Timothy McDermott's contemporary translation of Thomas's

9. McDermott, *St Thomas Aquinas Summa Theologia*, 119.

10. Ned Block, "Consciousness," in *A Companion to the Philosophy of Mind*, ed. Samuel Guttenplan (Oxford: Blackwell, 1994), 210–18, esp. 215.

11. Block, "Consciousness," 210–12.

account: "Higher animals must be aware of something not only when it is present to their senses but also in its absence, so that they can be prompted to seek it. So they not only need to receive, but also to retain, impressions of sense objects presently affecting them." This ability to retain sense impressions in the absence of the stimulus is called the *phantasia* in Latin, and often translated as "imagination."[12]

> In addition, [he says] animals need to be attracted and repelled not only by what pleases or displeases their senses but by what is useful or harmful . . . : the straws birds collect must look good for nest-building. So animals must be able to perceive a significance in things that is not merely an externally perceptible quality. In addition to their particular senses . . . for receiving sense impressions and their imagination for storing them, animals must therefore have an instinctive judgment [the *vis aestimativa*; also translated as "estimative power"] . . . and a memory [*vis memorativa*, or "sense memory"] for storing [them]. . . . Particular senses discern the particular sense-stimuli proper to them, but to distinguish white from sweet we need some common root sensitivity in which all sense-perceptions meet [the *sensus communis*—the "common" or "unifying sense"].[13]

In this last sentence Thomas is raising the issue that neuroscientists call "the binding problem." That is, how is it that we can put together the sound of a bark, the sight of brown hair, the sensation of soft fur, and the smell to recognize that what we have before us is a dog? This is considered to be one of the hardest problems in neuroscience next to consciousness itself.[14]

Thomas's *vis aestimativa* is particularly interesting for neuroscientific investigation. Joseph LeDoux writes that when a certain region of the brain is damaged (namely, the temporal lobe), animals or humans lose the capacity to appraise the emotional significance of certain stimuli.[15] This research is also relevant to Thomas's *vis memorativa*, the ability to remember the emotional significance of a stimulus. He tells of a patient of a French physician who had lost her abilities to create new memories

---

12. McDermott, *St Thomas Aquinas Summa Theologia*, 121.

13. McDermott, *St Thomas Aquinas Summa Theologia*, 121.

14. Ned Block, "On a Confusion about a Function of Consciousness," in *The Nature of Consciousness: Philosophical Debates*, eds. Ned Block et al. (Cambridge: The MIT Press, 1997), 375–416.

15. Joseph LeDoux, *The Emotional Brain: The Mysterious Underpinnings of Emotional Life* (New York: Simon & Schuster, 1996), 69.

as a result of brain damage. LeDoux reports that each time the doctor walked into the room he had to reintroduce himself to her, because she had no recollection of having seen him before. He regularly held out his hand to greet her, but one day when their hands met, she quickly pulled hers back, because he had concealed a tack in his palm and had pricked her with it. The next time he returned, she still had no recognition of him, but she refused to shake his hand. He had become a stimulus with a specific emotional meaning. She learned that his hand could cause her harm, and her brain used this stored information to prevent the unpleasantness from occurring again.[16]

For Thomas, the rational soul is what makes us distinctively human. He attributed to it two sorts of intellect, passive and active, and will. Active intellect is the power humans have, but not animals, of acquiring abstract information from sense experience and forming judgments. Passive intellect is a kind of memory—a memory of facts and ideas. Thomas attributed memory of events to the sensitive part of the soul. Neuroscientists now distinguish something like a dozen different memory systems. The two sorts that Thomas distinguished are both classified as types of declarative memory and involve the medial temporal lobe of the brain. The *formation* of long-term memory requires the functioning of the hippocampus.

The functions Thomas attributed to the active intellect—abstraction, judgment, and reasoning—are less well understood in neurobiological terms than those shared with animals. However, all of these higher human capacities depend on language, and a great deal of work has been done on the neural bases of language use. The third of Thomas's rational faculties was the will. This is the capacity to be attracted to goods of a non-sensory sort. As Anthony Kenny says, the will is "a power to have wants that only the intellect can frame. . . . We can say roughly that the human will is the power to have those wants which only a language-user can have."[17] Along with intellect, this is the seat of moral capacities. Furthermore, since God is the ultimate good, the will also accounts for the capacity to be attracted to God.

Neuroscience now contributes to our understanding of both morality and religious experience. I will take up morality below, but only mention here that selected areas of the prefrontal cortices are hypothesized

---

16. LeDoux, *Emotional Brain*, 180-81.
17. Anthony Kenny, *Aquinas on Mind* (London and New York: Routledge, 1993), 59.

to be concerned with unique human properties, such as the ability to anticipate the future and plan accordingly, and the ability to orchestrate one's survival deliberately, at the command of one's free will.[18] In short, what Thomas described as the "appetite for the good" appears to depend directly on localizable brain functions.

A number of neuroscientists have begun to study the role of the brain in religious experience and have shown particular regions of the brain to be typically activated. When asked to comment on these studies I always point out that if one is a physicalist, as I am, it is not surprising that brain regions are involved in religious experience; in fact, some regions would have to be.

In this section I have gone down one of the most detailed lists available of the human capacities that in the past have been attributed to the soul, but I have barely scratched the surface of the scientific work that has been done on each of these capabilities.

How to Defeat Reductionism

Neuroscientists call accounting for consciousness "the really hard problem." What my colleague Warren Brown and I see as the hard problem is that of reductionism. That is, if humans are purely physical, then how can it *fail* to be the case that all of our thoughts and behavior are simply determined by the laws of neurobiology?

Brown and I were convinced that reductionism had to be false. Philosophers and scientists such as Daniel Dennett and Francis Crick could be reductionists when it came to free will, morality, emotions, and so forth. But they never got around to applying it to their own thinking. If all our thoughts, including the ones they write in their own books, are determined by neurobiology, then in what sense are they true? In fact, do they even mean anything?

Brown and I agreed that while there were a lot of valuable resources for devising a *non-reductive* physicalist account of humans, no one had yet put them all together to make the argument against neural determinism. We have tried to do this in our book, *Did My Neurons Make Me Do It?*[19]

---

18. Antonio R. Damasio, *Descartes' Error: Emotion, Reason, and the Human Brain* (New York: Putnam's, 1994), 10–11.

19. Nancey Murphy and Warren S. Brown, *Did My Neurons Make Me Do It?:*

I will try to condense the important parts of our argument into this essay. The worry about neurobiological determinism is an instance of a broader thesis called *causal* reductionism. This is the claim that the behavior of all complex entities is determined by the behavior of their parts. This *is* the case in many systems we understand, such as mechanical clocks, which are designed so that the movement of the parts determines the behavior of the whole. The problem is that there has been a tendency throughout the modern period to assume that, when we turn to entities that are too complex to understand in detail, such as living organisms, they also must be determined by their parts. In the human sphere, the significant parts are genes or brain components, and so there has arisen a very sensible worry that the laws of neurobiology are inevitably determining all of our thoughts and actions.

When Brown and I started our work, we believed that the answer to the problem of neurobiological reductionism was to develop and apply a concept of downward causation or whole-part constraint. That is, if causal reductionism is the thesis that all causation is from part to whole, then the complementary alternative would be whole-part causation. Alternatively, if we describe a more complex system, such as an organism, as a higher-level system than its biological parts, then causal reductionism is bottom-up causation, and the alternative is top-down causation.

However, even if one uses top-down causation to argue against neural determinism, this still does not give an account of human *agency*. That is, how can we explain why we are not merely passive players influenced from "below" by our biology and from "above" by our environments? To answer this question, we needed an additional philosophical development: complex systems theory.[20]

Here are some of the essential concepts involved in this change. Several authors call for what might be termed a shift in ontological emphases; one has to give up the traditional western philosophical bias in favor of *things*, with their intrinsic properties, for an appreciation of processes and relations. So, for example, from a systems perspective, a mammal is composed of a circulatory system, a reproductive system, and so forth, *not* simply of carbon, hydrogen, calcium. The organismic level of description is largely *decoupled* from the atomic level.

Philosophical and Neurobiological Perspectives on Moral Responsibility and Free Will (Oxford: Oxford University Press, 2007).

20. Murphy and Brown, *Did My Neurons Make Me Do It?*, 42–67.

Systems are different from both mechanisms and aggregates in that the properties of the components themselves are dependent on their being parts of the system in question. Philosophers distinguish between internal and external relations. External relations do not affect the nature of the *relata*, but internal relations are partially constitutive of the characteristics of *relata*. An assumption of the predominant modern worldview was that the world is composed of *things* related to one another *externally*. Systems theory takes the relations among the constituent *processes* of a system to be *internal*.

Systems range from great stability to wild fluctuation. The most interesting are systems at the edge of chaos. Here systems have the freedom to explore new possibilities and may "jump" to a new and higher form of organization. In the process of self-maintenance, they create their own components. A living cell is a paradigm case. Its constitutive processes are chemical; their recursive interdependence takes the form of a self-producing, metabolic network that also produces its own membrane; and this network constitutes the system as a unity in the biochemical domain and determines a domain of possible interactions with the environment.

We reach a new level of complexity in systems that operate not on the basis of predetermined goals and feedback loops (for example, the homeostatic systems in an organism) but also have the capacity to select their own goals, and thereby adapt to new circumstances. These are called complex *adaptive* systems. When they also have some sort of memory, a way of storing information about what has or has not worked in the past, there is heightened ability for the system to increase its adaptation over time. One example is the storage of information in the genome that results in adaptation of the species. The capacity for memory in individual organisms brings us to the point of information and meaning. This opens the possibility of learning and the emergence of novel behavior, based in neural plasticity and the ongoing influence of events outside of the organism.

In sum, complex adaptive systems theory postulates that such systems become causal players in their own right, partly independent of the behavior of their components, selectively influenced by the environment, and capable of pursuing their own goals.[21]

---

21. Murphy and Brown, *Did My Neurons Make Me Do It?*, 67–90.

Moral Responsibility

At the end of my account of a few of the correlations between Thomas's soul capacities and neuroscientific work, I put off much discussion of Thomas's concepts of the rational will and morality because it was first necessary to provide an argument against human determinism.

Because the point of the previous section was to show how to defeat determinism, and also because of lack of clarity regarding the very nature of free will, I will consider instead the more amenable concept of moral responsibility. One needs to begin first with a philosophical account of the high-level cognitive capacities that are needed for morally responsible action. Second, one has to ask what *elementary* cognitive abilities go into each of these—a cognitive-science task. Finally, one may consider what we know so far about the neural processes that enable each of these more basic cognitive capacities. I draw here on the work of Alasdair MacIntyre for the philosophical analysis,[22] followed by some of my work with Brown on the second and third sorts of analysis.

Although there may be disagreement on how to define moral responsibility, the characterization given by MacIntyre in his *Dependent Rational Animals* has *prima facie* plausibility. Brown and I sum it up in one sentence: One is capable of moral responsibility when one has the capacity to evaluate that which moves one to act in light of some concept of the good. Here is how MacIntyre ties together the capacities that comprise practical reasoning:

> As a practical reasoner I have to be able to imagine different possible futures *for me*, to imagine myself moving forward from the starting point of the present in different directions. For different or alternative futures present me with different and alternative sets of goods to be achieved, with different possible modes of flourishing. And it is important that I should be able to envisage both nearer and more distant futures and to attach probabilities, even if only in a rough and ready way, to the future results of acting in one way rather than another. For this both knowledge and imagination are necessary.[23]

Brown and I analyzed his account of moral responsibility into five component cognitive capacities:

---

22. Alasdair MacIntyre, *Dependent Rational Animals: Why Human Beings Need the Virtues* (Chicago: Open Court, 1999).
23. MacIntyre, *Dependent Rational Animals*, 74-75.

1. A symbolic sense of self (as MacIntyre says, "different possible futures *for me*").
2. A sense of the narrative unity of life (as MacIntyre says, "to imagine myself moving forward from ... the present"; "nearer and more distant futures").
3. The ability to run behavioral scenarios ("imagination") and predict the outcome ("knowledge"; "attach probabilities ... to the future results").
4. The ability to evaluate predicted outcomes in light of goals.
5. The ability to evaluate the goals themselves ("alternative sets of goods ... different possible modes of flourishing") in light of abstract concepts of the good.[24]

Each of these five capacities involves a complex set of more basic abilities. There's no time to analyze each, so the first cognitive capacity, a symbolic sense of self, will serve as an illustration. The issue here is not the idea of *being* a self, but rather of having a self-*concept*. This concept arises, first, from the ability early in life to distinguish between self and non-self and, second, from the development of a theory of mind—meaning the ability to recognize others in the environment who have bodies of their own as well as thoughts and feelings.

Research by Leslie Brothers shows that we come well-equipped neurobiologically to develop and use what she calls the person concept. We have remarkable abilities to recognize faces and we have neurons that specialize in detecting bodily motions that indicate other actors' intentions.[25]

Patricia Churchland has examined some of the uses of the self-concept and concludes that the issue can profitably be recast in terms of the self-representational capacities of the brain, such as: representation of autobiographical events via the medial temporal lobes; control of impulses via prefrontal lobe and limbic structures; the ability to represent a sequence of actions to take next and to represent where one is both in space-time and in the social order.[26]

---

24. Murphy and Brown, *Did My Neurons Make Me Do It?*, 244.

25. Leslie Brothers, *Friday's Footprint: How Society Shapes the Human Mind* (New York: Oxford University Press, 1997), chap. 3

26. Patricia S. Churchland, "Self-Representation in Nervous Systems," *Science* 296 (2002) 308–10.

This is but one example of Brown's and my attempt to analyze the five factors we have isolated as the prerequisites for morality, and then to relate them to their neural substrates. Not surprisingly, two factors show up frequently throughout our analyses: sophisticated symbolic language and the capacity to direct one's attention to one's own cognitive processes—what Dennett calls "going meta."[27]

We see our analysis as a means of arguing that neuroscience *supports* the assumption that humans ordinarily have the capacity for moral responsibility. The structure of our argument, in brief, is as follows: If humans are to be morally responsible, they need (something like) the five cognitive capacities listed above. We know from observation that mature humans usually have these capacities. For example, developmental psychologists are able to chart and date the acquisition of a sense of self. The neuroscientific findings presented briefly here do not provide any significant reason to *doubt* these (apparent) facts of normal human functioning. If anything, they add to our confidence regarding the possibility of responsible action by explaining, as MacIntyre says we must, how this "form of moral life is possible for beings who are biologically constituted as we are."[28]

There are important conclusions to be drawn from my work here. First, if it is still possible to make sense of morality with a physicalist concept of human nature, then this goes a long way toward establishing, in light of current neuroscience, that physicalism is not necessarily reductionistic or deterministic. Then, if Christians are not essentially tied to dualism, non-reductive physicalism presents a preferable approach to theological anthropology. I have not provided adequate theological arguments for physicalism,[29] but on both scientific and philosophical grounds physicalism is clearly superior to dualism. However, the elimination of dualism would reopen a number of ethical debates for Christians, such as abortion and stem-cell research.

I repeat my one-sentence summary of MacIntyre's account of moral responsibility: it requires the ability to evaluate that which moves one

---

27. Daniel C. Dennett, *Elbow Room: Varieties of Free Will Worth Wanting* (Cambridge: MIT Press, 1984), 29.

28. MacIntyre, *Dependent Rational Animals*, x.

29. See Murphy, *Bodies and Souls?*, 24-30; and Nancey Murphy, "Historical, Scientific, and Religious Ideas," in *Whatever Happened to the Soul?: Scientific and Theological Portraits of Human Nature*, eds. Warren S. Brown et al. (Minneapolis: Fortress, 1998), 19-24.

to act in light of some concept of the good. I believe that he was intentionally vague in not specifying any particular concept of the good because *Dependent Rational Animals* is something analogous to a patch for computer software. The full program he meant to patch is worked out in what is now referred to as his trilogy: *After Virtue* (1981/1984); *Whose Justice? Which Rationality* (1988); and *Three Rival Versions of Moral Enquiry* (1990).[30] In *After Virtue* he provided an Aristotelian alternative to modern moral discourse, which trades in terms such as "rights," "rules," "utility," and so forth (as Gilbert Meilander has in his famous book, *The Theory and Practice of Virtue*[31]). However, Aristotle's project worked because of what MacIntyre calls his metaphysical biology, that is, his hylomorphic account of humans as constituted by prime matter "en-formed" by a rational soul. I believe, in contrast to Lee,[32] that this theory of human nature is incommensurable with contemporary metaphysics. Yet MacIntyre came to realize that no ethics can be done properly without some account of our biological nature, and that is what he provides in *Dependent Rational Animals*. Thus, while some reviewers have taken this book to provide a naturalistic morality, his overall position is explicitly theistic.

Conclusion

I will end with the issue of terminology regarding an acceptable Christian non-dualist account of humans. I generally call my position non-reductive physicalism, since that is the terminology most often used in philosophy. However, when I taught a seminar on human nature with my colleague, Veli-Matti Kärkkäinen, he objected to its apparent over-emphasis on the physical aspect of humans, and noted that another term sometimes used is "dual-aspect monism." But this is still an oversimplification of the biblical view of the multiple aspects of human life. He proposed "multi-aspect monism." An excellent way to describe this multiplicity is with Dunn's summary of Paul's position in his book, *The Theology of Paul the Apostle*:

---

30. Alasdair MacIntyre, *After Virtue: A Study in Moral Theory*, 2nd ed. (Notre Dame: University of Notre Dame Press, 1984); Alasdair MacIntyre, *Whose Justice? Which Rationality?* (Notre Dame: University of Notre Dame Press, 1988); and Alasdair MacIntyre, *Three Rival Versions of Moral Enquiry: Encyclopaedia, Genealogy, and Tradition* (Notre Dame: University of Notre Dame Press, 1990).

31. Gilbert C. Meilander, *The Theory and Practice of Virtue* (Notre Dame: University of Notre Dame Press, 1984).

32. This volume, chapter 5.

Paul's conception of the human person is of a being who functions within several dimensions. As embodied beings we are social, defined in part by our need for and ability to enter into relationships, not as an optional extra, but as a dimension of our very existence. Our fleshness attests our frailty and weakness as mere humans, the inescapableness of our death, our dependence on satisfaction of appetite and desire, our vulnerability to manipulation of these appetites and desires. At the same time, as rational beings we are capable of soaring to the highest heights of reflective thought. And as experiencing beings we are capable of the deepest emotions and the most sustained motivation. We are living beings, animated by the mystery of life as a gift, and there is a dimension of our being at which we are directly touched by the profoundest reality within and behind the universe. Paul would no doubt say in thankful acknowledgement with the psalmist: "I praise you, for I am fearfully and wonderfully made" (Ps. 139.14).[33]

---

33. Dunn, *Theology of Paul the Apostle*, 78.

www.ingramcontent.com/pod-product-compliance
Lightning Source LLC
Chambersburg PA
CBHW032236080426
42735CB00008B/885